KOREAN LITERATURE:
TOPICS
AND
THEMES

The Association for Asian Studies: Monographs and Papers, No. XVI

KOREAN LITERATURE: TOPICS AND THEMES

Peter H. Lee

韓國文學綜論

李崔洙 著

韩国文学忠公诉

李鶴洙 著

Published for the Association for Asian Studies by
The University of Arizona Press, Tucson, 1965

The publication of this volume has been made possible by a generous grant
to The Association for Asian Studies by the Ford Foundation

This text was developed pursuant to a contract between the
United States Office of Education and the American Council of Learned
Societies and is published with permission of the
United States Office of Education.

Project No. 35 of Research and Studies in Uralic and Altaic
Languages of the American Council of Learned Societies.

To my parents

千歲를 누리소서
萬歲를 누리소서
무쇠기동에 곳픠어
여름이 열어 싸 드리도록 누리소서
그 밧긔 億萬歲外에
또 萬歲를 누리소서

List of Abbreviations

AY: Asea yŏn'gu
CBTN: Chŏnbuk taehakkyo nonmunjip
CGTN: Ch'ŏnggu taehakkyo nonmunjip
CH: Chindan hakpo
CHB: Ch'oe Hyŏn-bae sŏnsaeng
  hwangap kinyŏm nonmunjip
CJTN: Ch'ŏngju taehakkyo nonmunjip
CM: Chayu munhak
CNTN: Chŏnnam taehakkyo
  nonmunjip
CTN: Chungang taehakkyo
  nonmunjip
HG: Han'gŭl
HM: Hyŏndae munhak
KK: Kugŏ kungmunhak
KKY: Kugŏ kungmunhak yŏn'gu
  (Ch'ŏnggu University)
KTN: Kyŏngbuk taehakkyo
  nonmunjip
KY: Kugŏ yŏn'gu
MH: Minsok hakpo
PNC: Yongjae Paek Nak-chun
  paksa hwangap kinyŏm kukhak
  nonch'ong
PPN: Paek Sŏng-uk paksa songsu
  kinyŏm pulgyohak nonmunjip
SG: Sasanggye
SGTN: Sŏnggyungwan taehakkyo
  nonmunjip
SHTN: Sinhŭng taehakkyo nonmunjip
STN: Seoul taehakkyo nonmunjip
SY: Sijo yŏn'gu
TH: Tongbang hakchi
TMY: Taedong munhwa yŏn'gu
YH: Yŏksa hakpo
YHS: Ilsŏk Yi Hŭi-sŭng
  sŏnsaeng songsu kinyŏm nonch'ong

CONTENTS

Preface

THE PURPOSE of this book is to study the vernacular genres of verse and prose in Korea. The sequence of the genres discussed is roughly chronological, and each chapter attempts to trace the birth and growth of the subject based upon both its outer and inner forms. Because of limited space and the intended use of the book, only those authors who contributed to the development of the genre under discussion are mentioned; hosts of minor writers are disregarded. This study attempts to be both factual and critical. Since conclusions on the *Saenaennorae* and *changga* are drawn solely from a small number of extant poems, chapters I and II list all Old and Middle Korean poems. Also, chapter X contains an unusually large number of authors because of the long history and bulk of existing writing in Chinese, a type of writing which enjoyed an unbroken popularity up till the end of the nineteenth century among some writers yet contributed iittle to the development of the Korean language.

The history of Korean literary history is short.[1] It was only after 1945 that Korean literature began to be studied extensively by Koreans themselves. But the accumulated scholarship during the short span of these seventeen years is amazingly vast. There are many controversial points, especially on Old Korean poetry, which have to be further studied and interpreted. Such topics as the drama and the *p'ansori* are yet to be explored. Every day new evidence is unearthed, and new theories advanced. A literary history of Korea by one author, which is at once comprehensive and authoritative over the entire field, is therefore almost impossible. I have, however, iried to consult the most important studies on each subject. For the convenience of the reader who wishes to pursue further the matters that interest him, I have appended, after each chapter, a select bibliography of the most important books, articles, and translations which have appeared by 1963. The most useful bibliography is the *Kukhak yŏn'gu nonjŏ ch'ongnam* (1960),[2] and I ask the reader to turn to this book for further information. The reader is also referred to my *Anthology of Korean Poetry from the Earliest Era to the Present* (New York: John Day, 1964) which includes most of the poems discussed in this book.

[1]For an account of the rise of literary history in Korea see my review of six histories of Korean literature in the *Harvard Journal of Asiatic Studies*, XXIII (1961), 172-182.

[2]Cf. Asiatic Research Center of Korea University, ed., *Bibliography of Korean Studies* (1961).

Dates have been supplied where possible on the first occurrence of an author's name. Characters for Korean names and terms occurring in the text are given in the glossary. Unless otherwise mentioned, all the Korean books are published in Seoul.

Chapters VII and VIII first appeared in *Oriens Extremus,* VIII (1961), 208-222.

This text was prepared under a grant from the American Council of Learned Societies in pursuance of a contract with the United States Office of Education, and I wish here to express my thanks to the ACLS and its Research Program in Uralic and Altaic Languages for their generous assistance. My thanks are also due Michael C. Rogers, Edward W. Wagner, and Burton Watson, all of whom have read the manuscript and made valuable suggestions.

Honolulu, July, 1964   PETER H. LEE

I. The *Saenaennorae*

The first notice of Korea appears in various Chinese chronicles: the *Chu-shu chi-nien*,[1] *Hou Han shu*,[2] and *Wei chih*.[3] We are told of nine tribes in continual strife for land and power from the Metal Age up to the beginning of the Christian Era. What strikes us forcibly, however, is not the petty squabbling of these nine tribes, but their essential unity in language and culture, especially in their love of singing and dancing. The *Chu-shu chi-nien* and *Hou Han shu* even tell us that Korean music was already introduced to the Hsia courts approximately 2,000 years before Christ.

Be that as it may, the Puyŏ, Koguryŏ, and Ye tribes were termed by Chinese historians "the people who enjoy singing and dancing." It was customary for the Puyŏ tribe to offer a sacrifice to Heaven during the first moon, and on that occasion the people assembled together and drank and danced for several days in a festival called *Majigut* ("Welcoming the Drum"). The Koguryŏ tribe was similar in language and customs to the Puyŏ. During the tenth moon, the offering of sacrifice to Heaven was made and there took place a major festival called *Saebŭlk* ("Dawn"). The East Okchŏ spoke a language quite similar to that of the Koguryŏ and had something in common with the Koguryŏ in their food, housing, clothing, and manners. The Ye, a branch of the Koguryŏ tribe, spoke the same language and offered a sacrifice to Heaven during the tenth moon; in the festival called *Hanbŭlkch'um* ("Dance to Heaven") the people drank, sang, and danced day and night.

The preceding paragraph based on the Chinese chronicles relates to the life of the northern tribes. Our source, moreover, informs us that in the south, the Mahan, one of the three southern tribes, offered sacrifices to spirits and gods after finishing sowing sometime during the fifth moon. The people flocked together for the occasion and danced and sang far into the night. Their dance was performed in this way: several dozen people stood in rows, stamping the ground; their hands and feet kept time with the music and the rhythm was like that used for the bell-and-clapper dance. They celebrated in the same way when the crop was gathered. The Chinhan tribe, another of the southern tribes,

---

[1]"Bamboo Annals," a chronicle of the state of Wei. Recovered from a grave in the third century A.D., it was subsequently lost, but was partly reconstructed from quotations preserved in other works.

[2]"History of the Later Han Dynasty," compiled by Fan Yeh (398-445).

[3]"History of Wei," in the *San-kuo chih* ("History of the Three Kingdoms"), compiled by Ch'en Shou (233-297).

had a large horizontal musical instrument somewhat similar in shape to a five-stringed lute.

The first recorded instance in which poems are used as means of incantation occurs as early as the first century A.D. In the section on the Karak state (42-562) in the *Samguk yusa* ("Remnants of the Three Kingdoms," c. 1285), we are told that during the third moon of the year 42 (the nineteenth year of Yuri, the third king of Silla), nine chiefs and more than 200 men climbed Mount Kuji to greet the sovereign, dug a hole at the summit of the mountain, and sang in joy the *Yŏng sin'gun ka* ("Song of Welcome"):

> O tortoise, tortoise,
> Show your head.
> If you do not,
> We will roast and eat you.

This is, according to the *Samguk yusa,* a sacred hymn, incantatory, coercive, and imperative in quality. We may conjecture that it was an extension of the ritual prayer used during the primitive era. The songs of this kind, however, are magic formulations such as make it impossible for us to determine their purpose and tone, even if we can read them in the original. For example, we must take it simply on the authority of the *Samguk yusa* that the song above is a joyous song of greeting, whereas the same authority declares that the song which follows shortly, though seemingly identical in detail and form, is entirely different in its purpose and tone, and is of secular rather than religious status. During the reign of King Sŏngdŏk (702-737), Duke Sunjŏng's wife, Suro, was taken out to sea by the Dragon King. The people, following the advice of a certain old man, sang as follows:

> Tortoise, tortoise, return the Lady Suro.
> Do you know the gravity of your sin?
> If you behave against our will,
> We will catch you in a net and roast you.

The quality of the earliest Korean poetry was thus religious or magical. We may conjecture that its norm was a few lines of simple language followed by a refrain. The language was incantatory, rich in its associative power and reference — much of which remains unclear to us — and in its rhythm and euphonies. It not only exerted a binding effect upon men, but upon the gods and spirits as well. It was, first of all, a means of communication between gods and men. The magical power of poetry was believed in to such an extent that it was supposed to please gods, help avoid natural calamities, bring rain and stop the winds, and promote recovery from diseases. The Greek equivalent of this idea was manifested in their drama, which was instituted in honor of Dionysus, a fertility god. The ancient Chinese idea of poetry was also essentially similar. A good example is the Emperor Shun's statement, supposed to have been made by him when he directed one of his men, K'uei, to gather the songs in current use, that spirits and men might be brought into harmony by poetry.

Furthermore, Chinese documents affirm that the same view was held by ancient Koreans as to the function of poetry: the Korean music, with its bright spirit, helped the growth of all relationships between Heaven and Earth.

Thus this ancient people realized the magical power and treated it with awe and reverence. Their primitive society was tribal and patriarchal, and primitive life was carried on in terms of communal value and significance. Poetry, music, and dance, the three vital elements in their religious service, were inseparable and indispensable. The love for song and dance was part of their mode of living, rooted firmly in communal belief. We must confess that from a scholarly viewpoint a complete and systematic history of the earliest Korean poetry is all but beyond a modern writer's capacity, owing to the lack of historical records. There are, except for fragmentary references in Chinese histories, no written records to which we may refer. Yet we may conclude that the earliest Korean poetry, insofar as we know it, was closely connected with Korean religion and was mainly composed of sacred hymns. Some scholars attempt to trace the original form of Korean poetry to the two songs mentioned above. But we must realize that these songs were later recorded by the historians for convenience in Chinese, following the Chinese metre and form. We cannot assume that these poems originally possessed their present form. In any case, this Korean poetry was a folk art that grew naturally from the life of the time. The subject matter was limited to praise of the virtue and excellence of gods and goddesses; it was not lyrical, but narrative. It did not deal with personal emotions and experiences, but with communal wishes and prayers. And since the art of writing was not known to these people, it did not have fixed forms.

In Korean histories, the first record of songs of Silla occurs in the *Samguk sagi* ("Historical Record of the Three Kingdoms," 1146),[4] though the *Samguk yusa* has something to say on this subject. When King Yuri (24-57) made a tour of inspection of the country in the eleventh moon, A.D. 28, he happened to see an old woman dying of hunger and cold in the open. He reproached himself, saying that it was his fault, if as king he was unable to feed the people, thus making the old and the young suffer to this extreme. He covered the old woman with his own coat and gave her food. He further ordered the civil authorities to find the widowers, the widows, the destitute, and the old and sick who could not provide for themselves and to give them food and shelter. When they heard this story, many people from the neighboring provinces came to Silla to praise the king. That year the grateful people composed the *Tonnorae*, which might be translated as "National Song."[5] To say that this

[4]This work was presented to the throne on January 25, 1146. For more on the *Samguk yusa* and *Samguk sagi* see chap. vii.

[5]*Tonnorae* has usually been read *"Tosolga"*. The term is something of a problem, but the word *tot* or *t'ŏ* is conjectured to mean "the people," "the land," and by extension "the tribe" and ultimately "the nation." For a detailed consideration of this term see Peter H. Lee, *Studies in the Saenaennorae: Old Korean Poetry*, p. 10 and note 46 on p. 132.

is the beginning of poetry and music in Silla means, of course, not that popular songs in Silla began in this period, but merely that the establishment of standard national songs begins with the *Tonnorae*. Though this song is communal, it represents in the history of Korean poetry a transitional form in which communal and narrative poetry developed into individualistic and lyric poetry.

Unhappily the earliest flowering of this lyrical poetry is known to us through the chronicles for the most part in terms of individual titles accompanied sometimes by the circumstances which prompted the composition of these poems; the texts in most cases have been lost. We have records of forty-one poems of the Silla period, five poems of the Koguryŏ period, and four poems of the Paekche period.

The first mention of the Silla songs begins with the time of King Yuri. The *Samguk yusa,* however, making references to the *Tonnorae,* further comments that the song had a structure and style called *saenae*. What is *"saenae"*? We may gather from many passages in the *Samguk yusa* and in the *Kyunyŏ chŏn* ("Life of the Great Master Kyunyŏ," 1075)[6] that *saenae* is not a name for a single poem, but rather a comprehensive term covering many poems. It is a genre, the norm of which can perhaps be traced in the existing Silla poems.

The various Chinese characters used to write *sae* and *nae* are used not for their original meaning—the combinations of two characters have no meaning in Chinese—but to transliterate a Silla word. We observe that the *saenae* music composed in the time of King Yuri and that composed in the time of King Naehae (196-230) have the same name, and that the *Tonnorae* of King Yuri is nothing but the name of a *saenae* piece of music. Thus *saenae* is a generic term which covers different songs with different contents composed at different times. Some compilers of histories have considered the various spellings to be entirely different names for different songs and have failed to recognize them as different transcriptions of the same word.

The word itself has been thoroughly investigated by Professor Yang Chudong. He concludes that *saenae* means "eastern river" or "eastern land" and that it came to be used in the sense of "one's native country." Thus *Saenaennorae* means Korean poetry in a broader sense, but when used as a genre term for Old Korean poetry, it covers the poems written from the beginning of the Silla dynasty to the end of the tenth century: fourteen poems in the *Samguk yusa* and eleven devotional poems in the *Kyunyŏ chŏn*. The name *Saenaennorae* was translated by scholars when they wrote in Chinese as *hyangga,* and it is by this name that these poems have subsequently been known. We prefer, however, to revert to the original Korean name.

In the kingdoms of Silla and early Koryŏ the conditions necessary to produce good poetry existed, and poets said to be of the first class succeeded one after another. But the poems which remain are comparatively few and the reasons for this are not yet quite clear to us. In the year 888, so the *Samguk sagi* informs us, an anthology of poems, odes, and elegies called *Samdaemok* ("Catalogue of Three Periods") was compiled by Wi Hong and Taegu by command of Queen Chinsŏng (887-897). But, alas, it was not handed down to posterity, probably because of the havoc of war. Nothing is known as to its form or its classifications; however, there are good reasons to conjecture that it had, from its title, a certain order in its compilation. One scholar even ventures to guess that the number of poems contained in this anthology may have amounted to more than a thousand. And another conjectures that the original texts of fourteen Old Korean poems in the *Samguk yusa* were probably copied from this anthology.

In the *Samguk yusa* as well as in the *Kyunyŏ chŏn* the texts of the poems were transcribed into Chinese logographs used either for their phonetic or logographic values. This system of transcription was called *hyangch'al*.[7] Historical sources tell us that this system was standardized by a scholar, Sŏl Ch'ong, around 692. Since Chinese characters are logographs, they can be borrowed for their logographic value in their original sense, even though the Chinese pronunciation of the character is not known. In Korea they were also used for their phonetic value to transliterate the Korean language. This was owing to the absence of any other system of writing in Korea until 1443.

Sŏl Ch'ong was a profound scholar, and he used this method of transcription primarily in deciphering the Chinese classics, which were very difficult for beginners to read and interpret. What he did was to insert auxiliary words between the Chinese character and indicate how they should be read in the Korean reading. In short, he made, so to speak, an *explication de texte*. And during the process of this explication he gave a logical systematization to the Chinese characters thus used. But it is held among specialists of today that this system was the product not of an individual genius, but of many people who used the characters in the same way for different purposes. We can trace this very easily in the texts of the poems themselves where the method of transcription is not uniform.

On the basis of the existing twenty-five poems, we may say that there are three forms: a stanza of four lines, two stanzas of four lines, and two stanzas of four lines plus a stanza of two lines. The first is the simplest form and occurs four tines. Many nursery rhymes, children's songs, and old folk songs retain this form; children's songs are still written in this form. The primitive religious songs and folk songs must have had a form somewhat similar, as it had the easiest and simplest structure and hence was easy to sing and remember. For this reason we may consider it the first fixed form of Old Korean poetry. The second form shows a middle stage in the structural development, and occurs three times. The third is the perfected and most polished form of all and was

---

[7]Also called *idu*. The term *hyangch'al* occurs for the first time in the *Kyunyŏ chŏn* (Ch'oe Nam-sŏn ed., 1954, VIII, 63) and *idu* somewhat later, in such works as the Postface to the *Hunmin chŏngŭm* (the Chŏn text, pp. 31a-b). Although some scholars insist that these are two different terms, others use them interchangeably.

the most popular form in Old Korean poetry. It first appeared toward the end
of the seventh century. It has two stanzas of four lines, where the main theme
is developed, and a stanza of two lines, which is called either a final stanza or
a refrain, in which a summary of a thought that has been developed is given
in the form of wishes, commands, or suggestions. This last stanza gives, so to
speak, a conclusion to the poem, at times in a very sophisticated manner, and
has an epigrammatic quality, memorable and quotable. Structurally, the ninth
line begins with an interjection, *aŭ* (sixteen times) or *aŭŭ* (once), whose
function in the poem is still discussed by scholars. As in other genres of
Korean poetry, the number of groups of syllables determines the accent and
rhythm in Old Korean poetry. Each line consists of one to five groups of one
to seven syllables, and the number of accented syllables generally corresponds
to the number of groups of syllables in a line.

Four-Line Poems

The *Mattung yo* ("Song of Mattung," c. 600) was composed by King Mu
of Paekche as a part of the stratagem to win Princess Sŏnhwa, the third daughter of the Silla king, Chinp'yŏng (579-632).[8] The *P'ungyo* ("Ode to Yangji,"
c. 635) is an anonymous ode written to praise the virtues of Yangji, a noted
priest and calligrapher. According to the *Samguk yusa,* this song spread among
the people when they helped Yangji carve the sixteen-foot-high Buddha statue
for the Yŏngmyo Temple. The *Hŏnhwa ka* ("Dedication of the Flower,"
c. 702-737) was written by a certain old herdsman. When Lady Suro, Duke
Sunjŏng's wife, asked for the azalea blooming on the cliff and nobody dared
climb to the top, this old man plucked the flower and dedicated it to the lady
with this song.

> If you would let me leave
> The cattle tethered to the brown rocks,
> And feel no shame for me,
> *I* would pluck and dedicate the flower!

The *Tonnorae* ("Dedication," 760) was written by Master Wŏlmyŏng, a priest,
poet, and member of the *hwarang,* leaders of the knights in Silla. In the year
760, on the first day of the fourth moon, two suns appeared in the sky and
remained for ten days. King Kyŏngdŏk, on the suggestion of his astronomers,
had an altar built to pray to the Buddha and waited for the priest destined to
perform this work. At that time Master Wŏlmyŏng passed by, and in response
to a request from the king he began the ceremony with this poem.

Eight-Line Poems

The *Mo Taemara ka* ("Ode to Knight Taemara," c. 692-702) was written
by Siro to praise his master, Taemara, a member of the *hwarang.*

[8]This tradition is incorrect historically. See my *Studies in the Saenaennorae,* pp. 103-105.

All men sorrow and lament
Over the spring that is past;
Your face once fair and bright,
Where has it gone with deep furrows?

I must glimpse you, Sir,
If I can, for an awesome moment.
My fervent mind cannot rest at night,
Far-off here in the mugwort-covered swamps.

In the first stanza the poet compares the spring to his master and laments that the once fair and bright face of the knight starts to wear "deep furrows." The last two lines achieve the culmination of his intense admiration for his master. Until he sees him again even for a moment, he cannot enjoy peace of mind. His anxiety for him will torment him even "in the mugwort-covered swamps."

In the *Wŏn'ga* ("Regret," 737) Sinch'ung reproaches King Hyosŏng (731-741) for breaking his promise.

You said you would no more forget me
Than oaks would wither before the fall.
O, that familiar face is there still,
The face I used to see and admire.

The moon in the ancient lake, it seems,
Complains of the transient tide, ebb and flow.
Your face I see no more, no more,
O, the vain world, it hates and harasses me.

The comparison of nature and man is brought in to emphasize the mutability of man's mind. The contrast is, in the first stanza, between the oak tree and a breach of promise. It is amplified in the second stanza, this time between the moon and the tide or between the moon and the tide and the king. The moon "complains of the transient tide," but the moon itself is changeable. Yet the poet realizes that the moon and the tide, however changeable they may be, are renewed and renewing in their cyclic changes, whereas man, once he has forgotten his promise, will never be reminded of it. Thus the scene of nature described here becomes the symbol not only of the speaker's deploring state of mind, but also of the contrast between his despair and the indifference of nature. In the eighth line, the poet exclaims: "O, the vain world, it hates and harasses me."

The *Ch'ŏyong ka* ("Song of Ch'ŏyong," 879) is probably the most famous of all Silla poems. The author of this poem, Ch'ŏyong, is one of the seven sons of the Dragon King of the Eastern Sea. He called himself Ch'ŏyong, so our source informs us, and married a beautiful woman. Seeing that she was extremely beautiful, an evil spirit transformed himself into a man and attacked her in her room while Ch'ŏyong was away. But Ch'ŏyong returned and wit-

nessed the scene, and calmly he sang this song, which so moved the evil spirit
that it went away.

> Having caroused far into the night
> In the moonlit capital,
> I return home and in my bed,
> Behold, four legs.
>
> Two have been mine;
> Whose are the other two?
> Two had been mine;
> No, no, they are taken.

A dramatic intensity is achieved by the change of tense in the verb form, from
"two have been mine" to "two had been mine" in the second stanza. Part of
this poem appears again in the choral dance of the Koryŏ period (lines 34-35
of the *Ch'ŏyong ka* of Koryŏ).

Ten-Line Poems

The *Hyesŏng ka* ("Song of the Comet," c. 579-632), written by Master
Ch'ungdam, worked a miracle: it cleared away a comet that had appeared in
the sky.

> There is a castle by the Eastern Sea,
> Where once a mirage used to play.
> Foreign soldiers came to admire this castle,
> Torches were burnt, rockets were fired.
>
> When knights visited this mountain, and when
> The moon zealously lit her lamp, and a star
> With a long broomstick swept a path,
> Someone said, "Look, there is a comet."
>
> The moon has already departed.
> Now, where shall we look for the long-tailed star?

In the second line of the first stanza a mirage is referred to, in the original, as
"the castle where Gandharva plays." The comet is variously described as
"a star with a long broomstick" which sweeps the path (for the moon) and as
"the long-tailed star." One commentator interprets the poem as a patriotic
song which eulogizes the blessings of peace in Silla.

The *Wŏnwangsaeng ka* ("Prayer to Amitābha," c. 661-681) was written
either by Kwangdŏk or by his wife.

> O Moon,
> Go to the West, and
> Pray to Amitābha
> And tell

> That there is one who
> Adores the judicial throne, and
> Longs for the Pure Land,
> Praying before Him with folded hands.
>
> Can the forty-eight vows be met
> If this flesh remains unannihilated?

In the first stanza the speaker addresses the moon and asks her to undertake a journey to the West where Amitābha ("the infinite honored one" or "one with boundless infinite life") resides. The second stanza amplifies the praise of the virtues of Amitābha. He not only possesses "boundless life," as his name suggests, but is also judicial. He passes his judgment from his "judicial throne." The last stanza presents a rhetorical question in which the speaker affirms that the flesh, which stands between the promised land and this world, must be annihilated.

The *Che mangmae ka* ("Requiem," c. 762-765) was written by Master Wŏlmyong in memory of his sister. The poem is built on a single image of separation through death, in the first stanza on the image of a crossroad (the road of life and death), and in the second on the image of the tree:

> We know not where we go,
> Leaves blown, scattered,
> Though fallen from the same tree,
> By the first winds of autumn.

The state of our existence is comparable to the branches of the tree. But the branches come from the same source, the trunk. Leaves which grow on the branches, however, when fallen from the branches, are forever separated from one another. We are, the poet says, like the leaves, and once we die, we are forever separated from our beloved ones. The theme is therefore skillfully developed by the simple figure of a tree—branches separated from the tree, leaves separated from the branch, and finally scattered leaves blown asunder. In the last stanza, the poet, as a devout Buddhist, hopes to meet his sister again "in the Pure Land."

The *Ch'an Kilborang ka* ("Ode to Knight Kilbo," c. 742-765) is a eulogy by Master Ch'ungdam written to praise Knight Kilbo, a member of the *hwarang*. This poem was known for its intense emotion and noble spirit, and King Kyŏngdŏk himself praised it highly. Unlike the other poems, this has no introductory note by Iryŏn, the compiler of the *Samguk yusa*.

> The moon that pushes her way
> Through the thickets of clouds,
> Is she not pursuing
> The white clouds?

> Knight Kilbo once stood by the water,
> Reflecting his face in the blue.
> Henceforth I shall seek and gather
> Among pebbles the depth of his mind.
>
> Knight, you are the towering pine,
> That scorns frost, ignores snow.

Internally, the first stanza ends with the third line and the second part begins unusually with the fourth line in the first stanza and continues to the end of the second stanza. In the last stanza, the poet's intense admiration for his friend is achieved by a single metaphor, the pine. Kilbo is "the towering pine,/ That scorns frost, ignores snow."

Another poem by Ch'ungdam, the *Anmin ka* ("Statesmanship," 765), is didactic. It is built upon a simple metaphor, an implied comparison of the government and the family. The last stanza, which was suffixed as a disconnected comment on the subject, is reminiscent of the remark of Confucius to Duke Ching of Ch'i when he said, "Let the prince be a prince, the minister a minister, the father a father, and the son a son." (*Analects,* XII, 11).

The *To Ch'ŏnsugwanŭm ka* ("Hymn to the Thousand-Armed Goddess," c. 762-765) by Hŭimyŏng, shows another instance of a miracle brought about by the power of poetry. This time the poetess implores the Thousand-Armed Merciful Goddess, painted on the north wall of the Left Hall of the Punhwang Temple, on behalf of her son who has lost his eyesight. The child regained his eyesight.

> Falling on my knees,
> Pressing my hands together,
> Thousand-Armed Merciful Goddess,
> I implore thee.
>
> Yield me,
> Who lack,
> One among your thousand eyes,
> By your mystery restore me whole.
>
> If you grant me one of your many eyes,
> O the bounty, then, of your charity.

Four lines in the first stanza describe in vivid language the external bodily preparation necessary for the prayer. The actual prayer is given in the following stanzas, lines five to ten. The calm and poised effects are achieved by the "if" at the beginning of the ninth line. "One," in "If you grant me one of your many eyes" in the same line, should be taken as an indefinite, rhetorical number.

The *Ujŏk ka* ("Meeting with Bandits," c. 785-798), by Priest Yŏngjae, is the most difficult of all Old Korean poems, partly because four words are missing in the text and partly also because the poet's symbolic language is loaded with many layers of meaning.

My mind that knew not its true self,
My mind that wandered in the dark and deep,
Now is started out for bodhi,
Now is awakened to light.

But on my way to the city of light,
I meet with a band of thieves.
Their swords glitter in the bushes —
Things-as-they-are and things-as-they-are-not.

Well, bandits and I both meditate on the Law;
But is that sufficient for tomorrow?

The first stanza, which resembles the beginning of the first canto of the *Commedia* in theme and imagery, introduces the first theme, that of journey. Night is not only the setting, it is a symbol of the poet's state of mind, which is that of a speaker who has "wandered in the dark and deep," in the world of illusion. After a long wandering in the dark, the poet is awakened to bodhi. He then starts for "the city of light." On the way he meets the bandits who also "wander in the dark and deep." This act of meeting them is, on the other hand, a source of enlightenment for himself and for the bandits. The swords that "glitter in bushes" finally aid the poet to comprehend the relationships between illusion and enlightenment. On the other hand, it is the enlightened poet who in turn enlightens the bandits. Thus the second stanza fully develops the theme of the polarity between illusion and enlightenment, which is already hinted at in the previous stanza. When the poet exclaims "Things-as-they-are and things-as-they-are-not," he has attained bodhi. The last stanza describes the constant harmony with the people, and the mind that is one with the wisdom of Buddha. Thus the poem is a revelation of the process of attaining bodhi, and it is built on the contrasts between night and day, darkness and light, illusion and enlightenment, things-as-they-are and things-as-they-are-not.

The eleven poems by the Great Master Kyunyŏ (917-973) are religious poems and are written in the Buddhist tradition. Kyunyŏ entitled his poems after the ten vows of Samantabhadra, with the exception of the eleventh poem, which is the conclusion. The themes of the poems are: (1) worship and veneration of Buddha, (2) praise of Tathāgata, (3) the search for and offerings to Buddha, (4) repentance for sins and retribution in this life for the sins of a previous existence, (5) rejoicing in the welfare of others and in the reward of virtue, (6) entreaty for the turning of the wheel of Law, (7) entreaty for the coming of Buddha among the living, (8) constant following of the way of Buddha, (9) constant harmony with the living, (10) dedication of one's merits for the salvation of all living beings, and (11) conclusion.

Although the eleven poems were inspired by the *Bhadra-cari-praṇidhāna* ("Vows on the Practices of Bodhisattva"), often the imagery is more striking and beautiful than in the Sanskrit original or its Chinese translations by Buddhabhadra (d. 429), Amoghavajra (d. 774), or Prājña. The sixth poem, which asks the Buddha to revolve the wheel of the *dharma*, is the most dramatic and beautiful of all his poems. The poem opens with a fervent prayer for "the sweet rain of truth." The second stanza goes:

> Dispel the blight of affliction
> Rooted deep in the ignorant soil,
> And wet the mind's field
> Where the good grass struggles to grow.

The mind is "the ignorant soil" which suffers from "the blight of affliction." It is the dried field "Where the good grass struggles to grow" because of this blight. The metonymic adjective "ignorant" modifying "soil" is the most convincing, because where the temptations of ignorance pervade there cannot but be "ignorant soil," and where ignorance reigns "good grass struggles to grow." If the rain falls over the dried, ignorant soil of the mind, the blight will be dispelled, the grass will grow, and the soil will bear the "gold fruit of knowledge." This harmonious state of the mind is expressed in the last stanza by the single beautiful metaphor of "a moonlit autumn field." The autumn field must be illuminated by the moon, since the bodhi-moon is a symbol for enlightenment. Thus the last stanza achieves a magnificent unity of tone.

Bibliography: the *Saenaennorae*

Chi Hŏn-yŏng, *Hyangga yŏyo sinsŏk* ("A New Interpretation of Old and Middle Korean Poems") (1947), pp. 8-51, 66-72.

Cho Yun-je, *Chosŏn siga sagang* ("History of Korean Poetry") (1937), pp. 32-87.

―――――――――, *Chosŏn siga ŭi yŏn'gu* ("Studies in Korean Poetry") (1948), pp. 1-60, 81-100.

―――――――――, *Hanguk munhak sa* ("History of Korean Literature") (1963), pp. 10-15, 26-43, 57-62.

―――――――――, *Kungmunhak kaesŏl* ("Outline of Korean Literature") (1960), pp. 79-89.

Kim Tong-uk, *Hanguk kayo ŭi yŏn'gu* ("Studies in Korean Poetry") (1961), pp. 1-168.

Lee, Peter H., *Studies in the Saenaennorae: Old Korean Poetry*, Serie Orientale Roma, XXII (Rome, 1959).

―――――――――, "The Importance of the *Kyunyŏ chŏn* (1075) in Korean Buddhism and Literature―*Bhadra-cari-pranidhāna* in Tenth-Century Korea," *Journal of the American Oriental Society*, LXXXI (1961), 409-414.

Ogura Shimpei, *Hyangga oyobi Idu no kenkyū* ("A Study of *Hyangga* and *Idu*") (1929).

Yang, Chu-dong, *Koga yŏn'gu* ("Studies in Old Korean Poetry") (1957).

―――――――――, *Kukhak yŏn'gu non'go* ("Studies in the Korean Language and Literature") (1962), pp. 22-29, 45-117, 127-259, 269-286.

. . .

Chang Sa-hun, "*Chŏngŭp sa* p'yŏn'go" ("A Study on the 'Song of Chŏngŭp'"), *Tŏksŏng hakpo* (1958), pp. 61-67.

Ch'oe Hak-sŏn, "Hyangga haesŏk sigo" ("A Study of the *Hyangga*"), *PPN*, pp. 1005-1026.
Chŏng In-sŭng, "Idu kiwŏn ŭi chae koch'al" ("A Study of the Origin of *Idu*"), *YHS*, pp. 643-652.
Chŏng Pyŏng-uk, *Kungmunhak san'go* ("Essays on Korean Literature") (1960), pp. 110-139, 140-148.
Chŏng Yŏl-mo, "Saero ilgŭn hyangga" ("A New Reading of *Hyangga*"), *HG*, 99 (1947), 12-22.
Hong Sun-t'ak, "Idu kyŏk hyŏngt'ae ko" ("A Study of the Cases in *Idu*"), CBTN, II (1958), 117-145.
Kang Sŏng-il, "Kodaeŏ ŭi hyŏngt'aenonjŏk yŏn'gu: idu ŭi 'chae' 'ko' rŭl chungsim ŭro" ("A Morphological Study of *Idu*, Especially 'chae' and 'ko'"), *Ŏmunhak*, 3 (1958), 96-123.
Kang Yun-ho, "Idu haksa yŏn'gu sŏsŏl" ("A History of *Idu* Studies"), *KK*, 15 (1956), 75-93; 17 (1957), 43-64; 18 (1957), 142-164; 19 (1958), 58-77; 20 (1959), 145-172.
Kim Chong-u, "Hyangga munhak ŭi chonggyojŏk sŏngkyŏk" ("The Religious Character of *Hyangga* Literature"), *KK*, 15 (1956), 62-74.
Kim Hyŏng-gyu, *"Chŏngŭp sa* chusŏk" ("Annotations on the 'Song of Chŏngŭp'"), *STN*, II (1955), 280-301.
Kim Ki-dong, "Hanguk ŭi pulgyomunhak non" ("Buddhist Literature in Korea"), *PPN*, pp. 171-197.
Pak Chi-hong, *"Kuji ka* yŏn'gu" ("A Study of *Kuji ka*"), *KK*, 16 (1957), 2-17.
Pak Sŏng-ŭi, "Kungmunhak kojŏn e nat'anan yu, pul, to sasang" ("Confucian, Buddhist, and Taoist Elements in Ancient Korean Literature"), *YHS*, pp. 261-295.
Song Chae-ju, "Hyangga e nat'anan 'si' e taehayŏ" ("On 'si' in the *Hyangga*"), *KK* 17 (1957), 94-104.
Yi Hye-gu, *Hanguk ŭmak yŏn'gu* ("Studies in Korean Music") (1957), pp. 238-291.
Yi Kŭn-yŏng, "Hyangga kot Sanoega (*sic*) ŭi hyŏngsik." ("The Forms of *Hyangga*, i.e., *Sanoega*"), *HG*, 105 (1949), 35-47.
Yi Nŭng-u, "Hyangga ŭi maryŏk" ("The Magic of *Hyangga*"), *HM*, II/9 (1956), 194-205.
Yi Sung-nyŏng, "Silla sidae ŭi p'yogipŏp ch'egye e kwanhan siron" ("The Transcription System of Korean in the Silla Period"), *STN*, II (1955), 62-166.
Yi T'ak, "Hyangga sinhaedok" ("A New Interpretation of *Hyangga*"), *HG*, 116 (1956), 3-50.
—————, "Idu ŭi kŭnbonjŏk haesŏk" ("Inferential Expositions of *Idu*"), *YHS*, pp. 525-530.
Yu Ch'ang-sik, "Hyangga e nat'anan 'si' ŭi munpŏpchŏk kinŭng kwa ŭmka" ("The Grammatical Functions and Sound Value of 'si' in *Hyangga*"), *KK*, 15 (1956), 36-61.

Translations

Lee, Peter H., *Kranich am Meer: koreanische Gedichte* (Munich, 1959), pp. 7-20.
—————, *Studies in the Saenaennorae: Old Korean Poetry*, pp. 52-101.

II. The *Changga*

It is a commonplace among literary historians that a study of Middle Korean poetry is extremely difficult. This is not because there is no lyric poetry in the Koryŏ dynasty, but rather because there are few written records to which we may refer about its origin and authorship, its form and content. It is therefore regrettable that we cannot systematically survey the literary life of the Koreans during 470 years of the Koryŏ period.

There are, of course, several inevitable reasons for this difficulty. First of all, there was no proper system of writing the Korean language in the Koryŏ dynasty. The result is that many poems of native and folk origin were sung or orally transmitted from time to time and were not recorded or preserved for posterity. While the preceding Silla dynasty invented the transcription method of Korean in Chinese, the *hyangch'al*, and the succeeding Yi dynasty the phonetic alphabet of twenty-eight letters, the *Hunmin chŏngŭm* ("Correct Sound in Teaching the People," 1443), the Koryŏ dynasty neither maintained the use of the *hyangch'al* nor substituted any other system. The invention of the *hyangch'al* was an indispensable stimulus which facilitated the rapid development of the polished form of the native poetic genre in Silla, the *Saenaennorae*, and many poets of genius used and perfected this form. The *hyangch'al* letters were used until the time of King Kwangjong (925-950-975), when Great Master Kyunyŏ wrote his eleven devotional poems in them, and as late as 1021 according to the inscription on the tower at the Hyŏnhwa Temple in Kaesŏng. The eleven poems by Kyunyŏ are, however, for philological and cultural reasons grouped with the fourteen poems written before 900 as Old Korean poetry. Thus, strictly speaking, when we enter the Koryŏ period, the use of the *hyangch'al* and of the genre of the *Saenaennorae* disappears. This is because skill in Chinese, which developed to a considerable degree toward the end of Silla, proved itself really capable of translating the Korean emotions and innermost feelings. The truth is that scholars found the *hyangch'al* inefficient; they called it a puzzle and abandoned it and the genre of the *Saenaennorae* that went with it. We see, however, in the *To ijang ka* ("Dirge," 1120), which is still written in *hyangch'al* letters, a transitional period, a period in which the *hyangch'al* letters still had supremacy. This is, indeed, a piece of Silla poetry, and it occupies an important position in the history of Korean poetry. Much later, in the fourteenth century, we see another example of this type in the two poems by An Ch'uk (1282-1348). Here the *hyangch'al* letters are used sporadically to transcribe not only connectives, but also refrains. It is evident from these examples that in the beginning of Koryŏ, where Silla culture still had influence, the recording method of the previous dynasty was still used; but in time Chinese began to infiltrate and was finally used in poetry to the exclusion of the *hyangch'al*.

The intensive study of Chinese literature and the encouragement of composition only in Chinese, which were responsible for other parts of our difficulty, demand explanation. The Koryŏ dynasty, which espoused Buddhism as the state religion, nevertheless imitated the fashionable conventions of government which were traditionally Chinese and were based on the principles of Confucianism, and leaned toward a policy of toadyism from the time of the Khitan invasions (993, 1010, 1018). As a result of the adoption of the system of the civil service examination, the two-corps system of government — civil and military — became effective in 958; only the civil officials chosen by this examination were occupied with state affairs. After seventy-five years of peace (1047-1122) Koryŏ declined gradually and suffered from the following disasters: internally, the opposition between ideas of independence and toadyism and between military and civilian corps; externally, from the invasions of the Khitans, Jurchens, Mongols, and Japanese. On the other hand, during the period of both peace and decline, Confucianism and Buddhism dominated the world of thought. A degenerated hedonism formed the basis of the upper-class culture, which attempted to disguise its troubles and worries and lived a secluded life. Loss of the independent spirit, worship of the powerful (therefore the study of Chinese literature only), and internal disturbances and foreign invasions all made scholars and historians reject the local culture. The government cared little about the cultivation of vernacular poetry and looked down on Korean poetry as "popular songs" or "unrefined language." Thus even the songs transmitted in *hyangch'al* letters, if they were not by members of the royal family or by famous officials or literati, and if they did not deal with national administration or current affairs, were not recorded in historical documents. Even the songs collected specifically as references for national customs and government affairs and those selected as materials for moral instruction were handled severely by historians and anthologists, who briefly gave their origins and omitted their texts.

Lastly, a handful of recorded poems were either lost in the course of time or were occasionally expunged by the Yi dynasty annalists and anthologists as "vulgar and obscene." As soon as the national policy was formulated, the Yi dynasty turned its attention to the poetry and music of the previous kingdom. This was a way to shake off the dust of Koryŏ and thus to make a new start for the Yi. The fall of Koryŏ was for this reason ascribed to Buddhism and all the vices accompanying it, and the new dynasty was built on rational ethics and strong political philosophy. But the choice of Confucianism as national policy had a deeper significance. The founders of the new monarchy were anxious to justify their revolution; the change of the dynasty had to be justified and praised. The traditional Confucian or pre-Confucian idea of the "Heavenly mandate" was called in for this purpose; it was Heaven that punished the virtueless Koryŏ dynasty, and General Yi Sŏng-gye, the founder of the new dynasty, was only its instrument to fulfill the mandate of Heaven; and in order to fulfill this mandate the state had to be based on Confucian principles. What went with this new policy was, however, a blind reverence for China and a respect for Chinese tradition. Thus when the Yi dynasty critics discussed tradition, it was the Chinese tradition which was the criterion for the judging of literature and the arts. Their criterion for Koryŏ poetry was a code of ethical practice based on Confucianism, and it was according to this interpretation of moral doctrine that one poem was termed "vulgar" and another "classic." During the period of the kings Sejong (1397-1419-1450), Sŏngjong (1457-1470-1494), and Chungjong (1488-1506-1544) the poetry and music of the previous dynasty were regulated and codified, and the critics concerned with this work condemned the popular poems of Koryŏ under three headings: vulgar, obscene, or Buddhistic. For instance, in the time of King Sejong, the *Hujŏn chinjak* (c. 1331-1332) came into question as "obscene" (1419) and *Muae*[1] as "Buddhistic and fantastic" (1434).[2] Among the three reigns mentioned, the Koryŏ poems suffered most during that of King Sŏngjong, when (1488, 1490) six of the existing poems were expunged or revised as injurious to public decency.[3] Scholars described them as "dealing with love between the sexes" or "pleasing men and women." It is true that the six poems deal primarily with affection between the sexes — probably because people of the lower class, driven to dire poverty and pain by internal disturbances and foreign invasions, became hedonistic praising love for love's sake if they did not become Buddhists renouncing the worldly life. But if we read these poems with a map of world literature in mind, we feel that they are good examples of the expression of the quality of experience, and we may ask ourselves whether they deserved to be treated contemptuously. It is, however, quite possible that the poems as we have them today are versions which have already been censored by the Yi dynasty scholars. It is therefore difficult for us to pass a definitive judgment on poems whose texts may have been altered by Confucianists of the time. But if the present versions are the same as they were in Koryŏ times, we are inclined to demand a justification for the patronizing attitude of the Yi dynasty scholars.

[1]*Muae* is a translation of the Sanskrit term *Apratihata,* which means "unhindered, without obstacle, resistless, without resistance, permeating everywhere, all-pervasive, dynamic omnipresence which enters everywhere without hindrance like the light of a candle." See Soothill and Hodous, *A Dictionary of Chinese Buddhist Terms* (London, 1937), p. 381b.

[2]*Sejong sillok (Chosŏn wangjo sillok* ed.), III, 1a; LXV, 21b.

[3]*Sŏngjong sillok,* CCXV, 1a; CCXIX, 4b; CCXL, 18b.

For the above-mentioned reasons, it is easy to comprehend the scarcity of collections of Koryŏ dynasty poems and of reference data compiled about them during the succeeding dynasty. Our only available sources are the section on music in the *Koryŏ sa* ("History of the Koryŏ Dynasty," 1451), a few scattered remarks in private literary collections, and reference books related to poetry and music compiled during the Yi dynasty (e.g., *Siyong hyang-ak po*). With only these materials we will try to investigate the state of Koryŏ lyric poetry. Historical sources record sixty titles of Koryŏ poems; twenty with texts (eleven poems in pure Korean, one in *hyangch'al* letters, three in *hyang-ch'al* and Chinese, two in Chinese translation, three with Korean readings of the Chinese translations and Korean connectives) and forty without texts (ten with a modified version in Chinese translation, eight prophetic songs with Chinese translation, twenty-two with titles only).

We have mentioned that the *To ijang ka* represents a transitional period between the *Saenaennorae* and Koryŏ poetry. Even in the *Chŏng Kwajŏng* ("Regret," c. 1151-1170) we see the aftermath of Old Korean poetry only with regard to the total number of lines, which amounted to ten (some give eleven); we do not see a clear stanzaic division as we do in Silla poems. The characteristic forms of Koryŏ poetry are the *changga* ("long poem") and the *kyŏnggich'e ka* ("*kyŏnggi*-style poem"). The former is so called because of the refrain recurring at intervals, generally at the end of each stanza. The refrain in the *changga* has several functions, but it is generally used to help achieve a certain mood in each poem, as in Provençal and Renaissance poetry. This character of the refrain is clear when we consider that the poems of the Koryŏ period were orally transmitted and that their origin lay in folk songs or in popular ballads. These poems were sung to musical accompaniment, and they found their place wherever men and women met together and entertained each other with songs. The refrain serves as a meaningless onomatopoeia of drum sounds or nonsense jingles to carry the tune and spirit of the songs—as in the *Tongdong* ("Ode on the Seasons"), *Sŏgyŏng pyŏlgok* ("Song of P'yŏngyang"), *Ch'ŏngsan pyŏlgok* ("Song of Green Mountain"), and *Isang kok* ("Treading Frost"). In the *Kasiri* ("Would You Go?"), however, it has clearly definable parts—an interjection, an imitation of the sounds of drums or other instruments, and a poetic phrase. Here the refrain seems to have a meaning which grew out of the poem itself, an ironical contrast between the speaker's distressed state of mind and the peace and prosperity of the time which others seem to enjoy. Some words in the refrains, as is the case with the *Kasiri,* might once have had a meaning, but in the course of oral transmission they lost their original meaning in the poems and came to be used as meaningless repetitions.

The refrain in the Koryŏ poems is an indispensable element in chain verse like the *changga*. It is by this refrain, rather than by other devices, such as *terza rima* in European poetry, that a poem is linked together, sometimes a poem consisting of several independent parts with different contents. This is the case with the *Sŏgyŏng pyŏlgok,* which consists of three sections, and the *Ch'ŏngsan pyŏlgok,* which consists of two sections. Each stanza in most Koryŏ poems can be read or detached as an independent unit apart from the entire poem. Yet, it is the refrain that links the individual units, so that each stanza in each poem can play its role in fully achieving the final effect. Several poems do not have stanzaic divisions, several different units being linked together. The *Ch'ŏyong ka* ("Song of Ch'ŏyong"), which consists of seven parts, including the poem written in 879 to praise Ch'ŏyong, is a good example of the *changga* tradition.

Upon scrutiny we distinguish two forms of the *changga:*

I 1) Each group (foot) in a line has two or three or four syllables, but most commonly three syllables.
2) Generally each line consists of three groups, but four groups are also possible.
3) There is no set number of stanzas in a poem.
4) The refrain occurs either in the middle or at the end of each stanza.

II 1) Each group in a line has two or three syllables, but most commonly four syllables.
2) Generally each line consists of alternating three or four groups, but four groups seem to be predominant.
3) There is no set number of stanzas in a poem.
4) The refrain tends to disappear from a poem.

Most of the long poems belong to the first class, but two poems, the *Isang kok* and *Manjŏnch'un* ("Spring Overflows the Pavilion"), belonging to the second class, already demonstrate the stage in which the *changga* gradually loses its fixed form and opens the way for the birth of a new genre, the *sijo,* in the Yi dynasty.

Strictly speaking, the *To ijang ka,* the *Chŏng Kwajŏng,* and the *Samo kok* ("Maternal Love") cannot be called *changga,* but they are traditionally grouped under this genre because of their dates and vocabulary. The *To ijang ka* is a royal poem of eight lines written by King Yejong. He praises the heroism of Generals Sin Sung-gyŏm and Kim Nak, who once saved the life of the founder of the Koryŏ dynasty in a battle against Chinhwŏn (892-935) of the Later Paekche dynasty. The *Chŏng Kwajŏng* is a poem of ten or eleven lines describing the bitter disappointment of a rejected courtier. During the Yi dynasty this poem, which was subsequently known by its musical tunes, *samjinjak,* was praised as an expression of loyalty to the sovereign. It was established as court music and was a requisite for all musicians.

The *Ch'ŏyong ka* is a dramatic poem of forty-five lines consisting of seven parts: prologue (1-6); the first chorus, praising Ch'ŏyong (7-24); the second chorus, describing the making of the mask (25-28); the confession of the demon (31-33); the second chorus, singing part of the Silla song of Ch'ŏyong (34-35);

a dialogue between the people and Ch'ŏyong (36-42); and the flight of the demon (43-45). This choral dance was performed at court on New Year's Eve to exorcise the evil spirits and demons from the country.

The *Ssanghwajŏm* ("The Turkish Bakery") purports to be by a *kisaeng*[4] and dates from the time of King Ch'ungnyŏl (1236-1275-1308). This was the time when popular songs and music flourished, with the encouragement of the king himself, who gathered musicians and dancers from all parts of the country for his entertainment. From the content of the poem, critics prefer to see it as a folk song of the day in the capital rather than as a poem of definite authorship.

> I go to the Turkish shop, buy a bun,
> An old Turk grasps me by the hand.
> If this story is spread abroad,
> You alone are to blame, little doll on the shelf.
> I will go, yes, go to his bower:
> A narrow place, sultry and dark.
>
> I go to the Samjang Temple, light the lantern,
> A chief priest grasps me by the hand.
> If this story is spread abroad,
> You alone are to blame, little altar boy.
> I will go, yes, go to his bower:
> A narrow place, sultry and dark.
>
> I go to the village well, draw the water,
> A dragon within grasps me by the hand.
> If this story is spread abroad,
> You alone are to blame, O pitcher.
> I will go, yes, go to his bower:
> A narrow place, sultry and dark.
>
> I go to the tavern, buy the wine,
> An innkeeper grasps me by the hand.
> If this story is spread abroad,
> You alone are to blame, O wine jug.
> I will go, yes, go to his bower:
> A narrow place, sultry and dark.

The poem consists of four eight line stanzas, the last two lines being a refrain occurring at the end of each stanza. Parts of the fourth and fifth and seventh lines in each stanza are an imitation of drum sounds carrying no definite meaning. (The translation uses a six-line stanza, because the drum sounds have been omitted.) The poem is in the first person throughout and the speaker narrates her adventures in four different circumstances. She uses the direct

---

[4] I have used the word "Turkish" somewhat freely here. Historically, the term *hoehoe* at this period denoted simply a Moslem, many of whom accompanied the Mongols into Korea in the thirteenth and fourteenth centuries. The *kisaeng* were female entertainers, comparable to Greek *hetaera*.

language typical of the time, and her determination finds expression in the last
two lines: "I will go, yes, go to his bower:/A narrow place, sultry and dark."
   The *Tongdong* is an anonymous long poem of sixty-five lines, divided into
thirteen four-line stanzas with a line of refrain at the end of each stanza.

> With virtue in one hand
> And happiness in the other,
> Come, come you gods,
> With virtue and happiness.
>
> The river in January
> Now freezes, now melts.
> The changing skies.
> I live alone.
>
> You burn like a lantern
> In the February moon.
> Burn like the bright lantern
> That shines upon the world.
>
> In the last day of March
> Plums are in full bloom.
> O magnificent blossoms,
> How I envy you!
>
> In April the orioles
> Come singing in pairs.
> My love, my bold knight,
> You forget bygone days.
>
> On the feast of the irises
> I brew healing herbs.
> I offer you this drink —
> May you live a thousand years.
>
> On a June day I bathe
> And comb my hair, and entice you
> Toward me like a pretty comb
> Floating just out of reach.
>
> For the feast of the dead,
> I prepare dainties of land and sea,
> And pray in this midyear day,
> That we may be always together.
>
> Under the full moon
> Of the midautumn festival
> I am lucky to be near you
> In the rippling light.

O season of chrysanthemums
In the ninth day of the ninth moon,
Drunk from wine, drunk from flowers,
Take care, my love, be well and strong.

In frosty October
You are handsome as the laden tree.
But once the tree is cut down,
What will become of my love?

On a long November night
I lie in an empty room
With a cold pillow and quilt.
O troubled heart, night without you.

In December I carve for you
Chopsticks from pepper wood:
An unknown guest holds them.
O bitter December!

The first stanza is a panegyric prologue and the following twelve stanzas are devoted to each of the twelve months of the year. Its traditional form of monthly division and its romantic content make it clear that it is a folk song of the time. The song was loved even in the Yi dynasty, and the annalist reports that the "Tongdong dance," together with the choral dance of Ch'ŏyong, was performed on New Year's Eve in the beginning of the Yi period.

The *Sŏgyŏng pyŏlgok* is a dramatic lyric spoken by a *kisaeng,* consisting of fourteen two-line stanzas. The second line in each stanza serves to keep the text to the musical tune and goes: "Wi tuŏrŏngsyŏng tuŏrŏngsyŏng taring-diri." The fifth, sixth, seventh, and eighth stanzas seem to have been popular in themselves, apart from the entire poem, and recur as the final stanza of the *Chŏngsŏk ka* ("Song of the Gong"). Stanzas nine to fourteen are most intense, with the speaker's plea to a boatman on the Taedong River not to allow her lover to cross the water, for "Once he has crossed that awesome water,/He will pluck another flower, alas." The poem became a political issue during the reign of King Sŏngjong and was officially condemned as "vulgar."

The *Ch'ŏngsan pyŏlgok* is an anonymous poem in which a lost lover takes a pessimistic view of life and tries every means to unburden himself of sorrow. He comes to the conclusion that wine is the best anodyne, and the poem ends, therefore, with an invocation and lines in praise of wine.

Let us live in the green mountain,
With wild grapes and wild thyme,
Let us live in the green mountain.

With cry and moan
The birds fly overhead.
Tremendous sorrow nests in me
And cries and moans after I wake.

The birds fly over,
My plough is blunt.
The birds fly crying
Across the water.

I have spent the day.
But in this deserted place
Where no man comes or goes
How am I to pass the night?

At what place is this stone thrown?
At what person is this stone thrown?
Here where no man loves or hates,
What if I stumble on the stone!

Let us live by the loud sea,
With seaweeds and cowries,
Let us live by the neighing sea.

While you are turning the corner,
While you are going to a kitchen,
Listen to the Tartar violin of birds
Perched on young antlers.

On the way to the sea I brew
Strong wine in a round jar.
A gourd-shaped leaven chases me and
Begs me to stay here; what now?

The text was not mentioned in any historical sources, but the *Akchang kasa*[5] ("Words for Music") records its text. The poem is written in eight four-line stanzas with the refrain at the end of each stanza: "Yalli yalli yallasyŏng yallari yalla."

The *Chŏngsŏk ka* is an anonymous hymn which sings of an unbroken line of kings and prays that the life of kings be coeval with Heaven and Earth. The poem begins with a three-line stanza of introduction and continues in five six-line stanzas. The poem offers a series of impossibilities, and then declares that, if these are ever resolved, "Then we part from the virtuous Lord," as the refrain in the third, fourth, and fifth stanza states.

The *Isang kok* is an anonymous love poem of thirteen lines with no stanzaic division, of which the third line is a refrain. This poem, together with the

[5]For this oldest extant anthology of Korean poetry see Peter H. Lee, "Popular Poems in the Koryŏ Dynasty as Described in the *Koryŏ sa* and *Akchang kasa*," *Oriens Extremus*, V (1958), 208.

Ssanghwajŏm, was mentioned in the "Sŏngjong Annals" (CCXL, 18b) as vulgar in content and as being that which pleases men and women.

The *Samo kok* is an anonymous short poem of five lines in all. Despite the scarcity of references, its vocabulary and syntax would seem to indicate Koryŏ origin. The poem is simple in structure and compares the difference between paternal and maternal love to that of sharpness between sickle and spade.

The *Kasiri* is another love poem spoken by a *kisaeng.* The poem consists of four two-line stanzas with a refrain at the end of each stanza. It is grouped with the other poems here for the same reasons as the *Samo kok.* This poem has much literary merit; its language is simple but intense, and it is filled with tender sentiments for the parting lover.

The *Manjŏnch'un* is an anonymous love poem of eighteen lines (four three-line stanzas, one five-line stanza, and a concluding line).

> Were I to build a bamboo-hut on the ice,
> Were I to die of cold with him on the ice,
> O night, run slow, till our love is spent.
>
> When I lie alone, restless, vigilant,
> Only peach blossoms wave over the west window.
> You have no grief, welcome the spring breeze.
>
> I have believed those who vowed to each other:
> "My soul will follow yours forever."
> Who, who persuaded me this was true?
>
> "O duck, beautiful duck, why do you come
> To the swamp, instead of the shoal?"
> "If the swamp freezes, the shoal will do."
>
> A bed on Mount South, a jade pillow, gold brocade,
> And beside me a girl sweeter than musk,
> Let us press our hearts together, our magic hearts.

The speaker is perhaps a *kisaeng,* abandoned by her lover and forced to spend long spring nights alone. She tries to console herself and, at the end of the poem, reveals her strong desire to follow him and possess him. The tone is frank and outspoken, and this is probably the reason for the condemnation of the poem by the Yi dynasty annalists.

In addition, historical sources list five titles as Koryŏ products whose texts are recorded in Chinese. One short poem by Yi Pang-wŏn (T'aejong, 1367-1410-1418-1422), the *Hayŏ ka* ("Song of Carefree Life," 1392), and one by Chŏng Mong-ju (1337-1392), the *Tansim ka* ("Song of Constancy," 1392), are commonly known not by their Chinese translations but by their Korean versions. The *Ch'ŏnggu yŏngŏn* ("The Eternal Language of Green Hills," 1728) gives a Korean version of the *Hayŏ ka* in the *sijo* form; it is difficult to determine how much of the original is retained in its Chinese translation or its

Korean version. The *Chahadong* ("Grotto of Purple Mist") was written by Ch'ae Hong-ch'ŏl (1262-1340), who lived in Chahadong and named his room the Chunghwa Hall. One day he invited an old man to his hall, composed this poem in Chinese, and had it sung by a servant. The *Yasim sa* ("Song of Deep Night") is an anonymous poem in Chinese which deals with the joy shared by the king and his subjects. The last poem, the *P'ungipsong* ("Wind among the Pines"), is an anonymous eulogy recorded in Chinese.[6]

The *kyŏnggich'e ka,* or *kyŏnggi*-style poem, is so called because of the refrain that begins "kŭi ŏttŏhaniikko?" and comes in the fourth and sixth lines of each stanza. The basic form is as follows:

$$3 \ 3 \ 4$$
$$3 \ 3 \ 4$$
$$4 \ 4 \ 4$$
$$3 \ 3 \ 4$$
$$4 \ 4 \ 4 \ 4$$
$$3 \ 3 \ 4$$

When we compare and analyze the poems written in this form during the Koryŏ period and later imitations written in the subsequent dynasty, we note the following characteristics:

1. Generally each group (foot) in a line has three or four syllables.
2. Generally each line consists of three groups, but one four-group line occurs in each stanza.
3. Each stanza always consists of six lines.
4. Each stanza can be divided into two parts.
5. Generally each poem consists of five to eight stanzas.[7]

We have three poems of this type as Koryŏ products, the *Hallim pyŏlgok* ("Song of Confucian Scholars," c. 1214-1259), by Confucian scholars, and the *Kwandong pyŏlgok* ("Song of the Diamond Mountains," c. 1330) and *Chukkye pyŏlgok,* by An Ch'uk. Texts are either in *hyangch'al* and Chinese (*Kwandong* and *Chukkye pyŏlgok*) or in Korean and Chinese (*Hallim pyŏlgok*), and are characterized by the cataloguing of things. These poems are products of a mature period of aristocratic culture and reflect the leisurely life of scholars hidden in the mountains far from internal disturbances or foreign invasions. The contents of the poems are therefore Epicurean or Taoist, and their tone is dignified and quiet, composed and learned. Later imitations during the Yi dynasty by Confucianists — the last of which is by Kwŏn Ho-mun (1532-1587) — are mostly finger-exercises loaded with dense allusiveness and have little literary merit.

[6]In addition, in the fourth chapter of the *Ikchae nan'go* (1363), a collection of writings of Yi Che-hyŏn (1287-1367), eleven poems are translated into Chinese in a four-line stanza of seven-word verse. Among the eleven, outline translations of seven poems are copied in the *Koryŏ sa;* one poem is a translation of part of the "Song of P'yŏng-yang"; and three are translations of unknown poems of folk origin. See *Ikchae nan'go,* in the *Yŏgye myŏnhyŏn chip* (1959), IV, 12a-14a.

[7]Some poems, however, demonstrate the following characteristics: (1) generally each line consists of four groups, (2) there is no set number of lines in a stanza, (3) division in the stanza tends to disappear, and (4) generally each poem consists of several stanzas.

Bibliography: the *Changga*

Chi Hŏn-yŏng, *Hyangga yŏyo sinsŏk* (1947), pp. 52-56, 75-128.
Cho Yun-je, *Chosŏn siga sagang* (1937), pp. 91-115, 129-157.
—————————, *Chosŏn siga ŭi yŏn'gu* (1948), pp. 101-115.
—————————, *Hanguk munhak sa* (1963), pp. 78-94, 132-141.
—————————, *Kungmunhak kaesŏl* (1960), pp. 89-109.
Kim Sa-yŏp, *Kungmunhak sa* ("History of Korean Literature") (1956) pp. 233-293. (1956), 94-115
Lee, Peter H., "Popular Poems in the Koryŏ Dynasty as Described in the *Koryŏ sa* and *Akchang kasa," Oriens Extremus* V (1958), 202-227.
Yang Chu-dong, *Yŏyo chŏnju* ("Studies in Middle Korean Poetry") (1947).
—————————, *Kukhak yŏn'gu non'go* (1962), pp. 117-126, 260-269.

. . .

Ch'oe Chŏng-yŏ, "Koryŏ ŭi sogak kasa non'go" ("The Texts of Koryŏ Popular Songs"), *CJTN,* IV (1963), 7-48.
Chang Chi-yŏng, "Yennorae ilki" ("A New Reading of Some Classical Poems"), *HG,* 110 (1955), 12-18; 111, 3-11.
Chang Sa-hun, *"Sŏgyŏng Pyŏlgok," HG,* 113 (1955), 13-21.
—————————, *"P'ungipsong," PNC,* pp. 495-508.
Chŏng Pyŏng-uk, *Kungmunhak san'go* (1960), pp. 149-159.
Kim Tong-uk, *"Siyong hyangak po* kasa ŭi paegyŏngjŏk yŏn'gu" ("The Background of the Texts in the *Siyong hyangak po"), CH,* 17 (1955), 103-186.
Nam Kwang-u, *Kugŏhak nonmunjip* ("Essays in the Korean Language") (1962), pp. 329-346.
Pang Chong-hyŏn, *"Akhak kwebŏm e taehayŏ"* ("On the 'Canon of Music'"), *Kukhak,* 3 (1947), 13-15.
Sŏ Su-saeng, "Koryŏ kayo ŭi yŏn'gu" ("A Study of Koryŏ Popular Songs"), *KTN,* V (1962), 277-325.
Yi Chu-hwan, *"Siyong mubo* haeje" ("Introduction to the *Siyong mubo"), Minsok hakpo,* 1, (1956), 189-194.
Yi Hye-gu, *"Akhak kwebŏm* yŏkchu" ("Annotations on the 'Canon of Music'"), *TH,* II (1955), 209-285.
Yi Ka-wŏn, *"Chŏng Kwajŏng* kok ŭi yŏn'gu" ("A Study of 'Regret'"), *Sŏnggyun,* 4 (1953), 70-80.
Yi Kŭn-yŏng, "Koryŏ Yejong ŭi *To ijang ka* haedok" ("A Reading of the 'Dirge' by King Yejong of Koryŏ"), *HG,* 101 (1947), 44-53.
Yi Myŏng-gu, *"Kyŏnggich'e ka* ŭi hyŏngsŏng kwajŏng sogo" ("The Development of the *kyŏnggi*-style Verse"), *SGTN,* V (1960), 25-63.
—————————, *"Kyŏnggi-ch'e ka* ŭi yŏksajŏk koch'al" ("The Historical Character of *kyŏnggi*-style Verse"), *TMY,* I (1963), 77-138.
Yi Nŭng-u, "Koryŏ siga ui sŏngkyŏk kogu: Yŏdae ŭi paeksong ŭi norae yŏn'gu" ("Characteristics of Koryŏ Poems, Especially Their Folk Origin"), *KK,* 14 (1955), 1-19.
Yŏnhŭi University Far Eastern Institute, *Siyong hyangak po* (1954).

Translations

Lee, Peter H., *Kranich am Meer,* pp. 21-33.
—————————, *Anthology of Korean Poetry* (New York, 1964), pp. 51-62.

III. The *Hunmin chŏngŭm*

The Korean alphabet, the *Hunmin chŏngŭm,* was invented by the great King Sejong[1] himself. He was the first Korean ruler to realize that the art of writing should be accessible to the common people. The thought of devising a new alphabet to meet the needs of the people was in his mind from the time of his enthronement. In the second year of his reign, therefore, the king called together the leading scholars in the Hall of Scholars (Chiphyŏnchŏn)[2] and ordered them to study the phonetics of Chinese and other oriental languages. Finally, in the twelfth moon of the year 1443,[3] the king succeeded in inventing a phonetic script consisting of seventeen consonants and eleven vowels. The Preface to the *Hunmin chŏngŭm* by the king reads: "Since our national language differs from Chinese and has no affinity with written Chinese, our people are unable to express what they wish. Having compassion upon our people in this situation, we have, therefore, devised a new writing of twenty-eight letters so that our people may readily learn it and use it in their daily affairs." The motive of the invention was therefore the king's great love of the common people and his wish to provide them with a means of expressing their speech and thoughts in writing. Indeed, Koreans were in great need of letters with which to write their own language.

Study was, however, continued for a further three years before the new alphabet was published as we have it today. King Sejong not only had his officials learn the new alphabet in order to test its practicability, but ordered Ch'oe Hang (1409-1474) and others in the Hall of Scholars to translate the *Ku-chin yün-hui* into Korean, using the new letters. Also, he ordered Kwŏn Che (1387-1445) and others to compose the *Yongbi ŏch'ŏn ka* ("Hymns to Flying Dragons in Heaven"), the first literary work in the new alphabet. This great eulogy-cycle, consisting of 125 cantos, was completed and presented to the

---

[1] King Sejong was born May 7, 1397; he ascended the throne September 7, 1418, and died March 30, 1450.

[2] "Hall of Scholars" or "Hall of Academicians," the *Chiphyŏnchŏn* existed, under different names, in the three kingdoms and Koryŏ. In 1420 King Sejong made it the center of learning and compilation. It was abolished in 1456 by tyrant Sejo. The members of the Hall prepared the royal lectures, compiled the "veritable records," drafted royal decrees, and made research into the ancient institutions of China and Korea. See *Chŭngbo munhŏn pigo,* CCXXI, 1a ff, 26a-b, esp. 3a; *Koryŏ sa* (Tongbanghak yŏn'guso ed., 1955), LXXVI, 27b-30a; *Sejong sillok,* VII, 30a.

[3] The *Sejong sillok,* which is the only source for this information, reads: "During this moon (i.e., the twelfth moon) the king invented the Korean alphabet consisting of twenty-eight letters" (*Chosŏn wangjo sillok* ed., CII, 42a). The twelfth moon of 1443 corresponds in the Western calendar to the period between December 21, 1443 and January 19, 1444.

throne on May 11, 1445. After nearly three years of testing of the practicability of the *Hunmin chŏngŭm* did the king allow its publication, in the autumn of 1446.[4]

There are altogether six versions of the *Hunmin chŏngŭm*. An authentic copy of the original edition was discovered in 1940 in North Kyŏngsang province. This copy was owned by the late Chŏn Hyŏng-p'il. The Chŏn text consists of thirty-three sheets arranged as follows:

Preface, by King Sejong..(1a)
The *Yeŭi*, by King Sejong
    1) Values of sounds..(1a-3b)
    2) Usage of the letters....................................(3b-4a)
The *Haerye* ("Explanatory Notes and Examples of Usage"),
    by Chŏng In-ji, Ch'oe Hang and others.................(5a-30b)
    1) Formation of the letters ....(5a-18b)
    2) Initial sounds...(18b-19b)
    3) Medial sounds..(19b-21b)
    4) Final sounds ....(21b-24b)
    5) Compound letters ....(24b-28b)
    6) Examples of usage....................................(28b-30b)
Postface, by Chŏng In-ji..(30b-33b)

The *Haerye* states that the letters are shaped according to the forms of the organs of speech. While the seventeen consonants are designed to represent the shapes and movements of the organs of speech, the eleven vowels are said to represent Heaven, Earth, and Man, and their combinations and relationships. Among the twenty-eight letters, four letters disappeared in the course of time: ㅸ (bilabial fricative) became obsolete between 1420 and 1450; △ (alveolar fricative) began to be obsolete by the middle of the sixteenth century; ㆆ (glottal) disappeared in the time of King Sejong; ㆁ (nasal velar) merged with the consonant ㅇ and disappeared in the seventeenth century.

The *han'gŭl* ("The Korean Alphabet") is "intricate and simple, mystical and effective" and "perhaps the most scientific system of writing in general use in any country," say Reischauer and Fairbank.[5] This system of writing is so scientific and easy to learn that it has remained virtually unchanged for five centuries. It has been proven to be the most adequate system of transcribing the Korean language. Chŏng In-ji (1397-1478) was right when he said in his Postface (32a) that "the *han'gŭl* is able to make a clear distinction between surd and sonant and to record music and song. It is good for any practical use and can even describe exactly the sound of the wind, the whoop of cranes, the crowing of cocks, and the barking of dogs." It is for this reason that *Der Grosse Herder* (V, 685) calls the *han'gŭl* "the easiest script in the world and the only alphabet in the Far East."

---

[4]*Sejong sillok*, CXIII, 36b-37b.
[5]*East Asia: The Great Tradition* (Boston, 1960), p. 435.

Bibliography: the *Hunmin chŏngŭm*

Ch'oe Hyŏn-bae, *Koch'in han'gŭl kal* ("Studies in Korean Phonology") (rev. ed.; 1961).
Hŏ Ung, *Chungse kugŏ yŏn'gu* ("Studies in Middle Korean") (1963).
Hong Ki-mun, *Chŏngŭm paltal sa* ("History of the Korean Alphabet") (2 vols.; 1946).
Kim Hyŏng-gyu, *Kugŏsa yŏn'gu* ("Studies in the Korean Language") (1962), pp. 261-371.
Kim Min-su, *Chuhae Hunmin Chŏngŭm* ("Annotated *Hunmin chŏngŭm*") (1957).
Kim Yun-gyŏng, *Saero chiŭn kugŏhak sa* ("A New History of the Korean Language") (1963).
Nam Kwang-u, *Kugŏhak nonmunjip* ("Essays in the Korean Language") (1962), pp. 13-122, 289-305.
Ogura Shimpei, *Chosŏn gogaku shi* ("History of the Korean Language") (Tokyo, 1940), pp. 69-91, 106-107, 112-115, 146-148, 159-169.
Pang Chong-hyŏn. *Hunmin chŏngŭm t'ongsa* ("History of the *Hunmin chŏngŭm*") (1948).
Yi Ki-mun, *Kugŏ p'yogipŏp ŭi yŏksajŏk yŏn'gu* ("Historical Studies in the Korean Writing System") (1963).
Yi Sang-baek, *Han'gŭl ŭi kiwŏn* ("The Origin of the Korean Alphabet") (1957).
Yi Sung-nyŏng. *Ŭmunnon yŏn'gu* ("Studies in Korean Phonology") (1958).
_____, *Kugŏhak non'go* ("Essays in the Korean Language") (1960), pp. 1-175, 231-260.
_____, *Chungse kugŏ munpŏp* ("Middle Korean Grammar") (1961).
Yu Ch'ang-don, *Ŏnmunji chuhae* ("Annotated *Ŏnmunji*") (1958).
Yu Yŏl, *P'urihan Hunmin chŏngŭm* ("Annotated *Hunmin chŏngŭm*") (1948).

. . .

Chŏng In-sŭng, "*Hunmin chŏngŭm* ŭi yŏnhyŏk" ("History of the *Hunmin chŏngŭm*"), *HG*, 98 (1946), 28-31.
Kim Tong-uk, "Chŏngŭmch'ŏng simal" ("History of the Chŏngŭmch'ŏng, Bureau of the Korean Alphabet"), *STN*, V (1957), 109-126.
Kim Yun-gyŏng, "*Hunmin chŏngŭm* e taehan myŏt kaji koch'al" ("Some Observations on the *Hunmin chŏngŭm*"), *YHS*, pp. 191-203.
Pang Chong-hyŏn, "*Hunmin chŏngŭm* kwa *Hunmong chahoe* wa ŭi pigyo" ("A Comparison of the *Hunmin chŏngŭm* and *Hunmong chahoe*"), *Kukhak*, 2 (1947), 10-18.
Yi Kang-no, "*Hunmin chŏngŭm* pyŏnch'ŏn ŭi iltan" ("One Aspect in the Development of the *Hunmin chŏngŭm*"), *HG*, 119 (1956), 10-17.
Yi Kwang-nin, "Sejong cho ŭi Chiphyŏnchŏn" ("The Hall of Scholars during the Reign of King Sejong"), *CHB*, pp. 157-176.
Yi Sung-nyŏng, "Sejong ŭi ŏnŏ chŏngch'aek e kwanhan yŏn'gu: t'ŭkhi unsŏ p'yŏnch'an kwa *Hunmin chŏngŭm* chejŏng kwaŭi kwan'gye rŭl chungsim ŭro hayŏ" ("King Sejong's Policy on the Korean Language, Especially with Regard to the Relations between the Compilation of Rhyming Dictionaries and the *Hunmin chŏngŭm*"), *AY*, I/2 (1958), 29-81.

IV. Early Yi Dynasty Eulogies: the *Akchang*

According to the Confucian canon, rites and music are the two indispensable means by which a virtuous ruler administers his state. Rites teach the people the patterned sense of community, order, and coherence in the hierarchies of society; music cultivates moral virtue in, and regulates the feelings of, the people. Rulers of Korean kingdoms, as in China, laid a due emphasis on both rites and music, mainly for their didactic function. It is no wonder, then, that the Yi dynasty, which rejected Buddhism and Taoism as subversive of public morality and adopted Confucianism as its official political philosophy, should re-examine the ritual and official music of the previous kingdom.

We have already discussed the activities of the first rulers of the Yi in their attempt to regulate and codify the existing songs and music according to Confucian principles. The popular Koryŏ songs which began to be used as court music from the time of King Ch'ungnyŏl—chiefly to entertain the court and foreign envoys on official occasions—became the objects of this literary inquisition. The new dynasty also directed the composition of court music clearly patterned after the Chinese models. The texts of the new court music written for use in the ancestral temple and official ceremonies were called *akchang*. The aims of composing such *akchang* were twofold: to justify the revolution and to emphasize the legitimacy of the new dynasty; and to praise the virtues and merits of its founder. As might be expected, the authors were all meritorious subjects who assisted in the revolution and who framed and executed the policy of the new government. Their eulogies remained a literature of the privileged class, and the forms they used for their composition disappeared soon after the end of the fifteenth century.

The first compositions of this kind, the *Monggŭmch'ŏk* ("Dream of the Golden Ruler") and *Suborok* ("Upon Receiving the Auspicious Diagram"), were presented to the throne by Chŏng To-jŏn (d. 1398) in 1393. The former is in irregular meters, in the *Ch'u tz'u* style; the latter consists of fourteen four-word lines. Chŏng further wrote four poems to praise the cultural accomplishments of King T'aejo and three to hymn his military genius. Among the military poems, the *Napssi ka* ("Song of Naɣačn," 1393) has as its theme the repulse of Naɣačn (1362)[1] and the *Chŏng tongbang kok* ("Pacification of the

---

[1]For an account of Naɣačn, who died August 31, 1388, see Henry Serryus, "Mongols Ennobled during the Early Ming," *Harvard Journal of Asiatic Studies*, XXII (1959), 212.

East") the return of King T'aejo's army from Wihwa Island, in the Yalu River. The texts of both hymns are recorded in the *T'aejo sillok* ("T'aejo Annals," 1413).

Kwŏn Kŭn (1352-1409), Pyŏn Kye-ryang (1369-1430), Ha Yun, and Yun Hoe (1380-1436) exerted their energy to celebrate the deeds and lofty virtues of the founder, to praise the new institutions, and to sing of the peace and prosperity they were enjoying.

The first in a series of poems which describe the beauty of Seoul, the new capital, is the *Sindo ka* ("Song of the New Capital," 1394), by Chŏng To-jŏn. In 1398 Chŏng wrote another hymn, the *Sindo p'algyŏng si* ("Eight Scenes of the New Capital"), in four stanzas of six-word verse. Kwŏn Kŭn and Ha Yun joined in the praise of Seoul, but a better poem in this vein is the *Hwasan pyŏlgok* ("Song of Mount Hwa," 1425), by Pyŏn Kye-ryang, which praises the capital and the king's benevolent government in eight stanzas.

Early Yi dynasty eulogies are written in three forms: in the traditional Chinese verse forms; in the Chinese verse forms and Korean connectives; and in the *kyŏnggi*-style form (see chap. ii). The poems belonging to the first class adopted the forms used in the dynastic hymns in the *Book of Songs*. The *Napssi ka, Ponghwang ŭm* ("Hymn to the Phoenix," c. 1401-1446), and *Pukchŏn* ("North Hall," revised in 1490) are examples of the second type. The *Hwasan pyŏlgok, Oryun ka* ("Song of the Five Relationships," 1419), *Yŏn hyŏngje kok* ("Brothers at the Feast," 1432), and *Sangdae pyŏlgok* ("Song of the Censorate," 1419) are written in the *kyŏnggi*-style form. A variant of the *kyŏnggi*-style form is used in such poems as the *Chŏng tongbang kok, Sindo ka, Yurim ka* ("Song of Confucian Scholars," 1419), *Sŏngdŏk ka* ("Song of August Virtue," 1420), *Ch'uksŏngsu* ("Long Live the King," 1420), and *Kam kunŭn* ("Song of Royal Favor," c. 1450).

The compilation of the *Yongbi ŏch'ŏn ka* (see chap. iii) was the culmination of literary activities in the early Yi Dynasty. This anthology, consisting of 125 cantos, was compiled and edited by the leading philologists in the Hall of Scholars and presented to the throne in 1445. The objectives of the compilation were fourfold: (1) to recount the difficulty of the vast royal works of the founders and their ancestors as well as the circumstances of the founding of the dynasty; (2) to remind future monarchs of the difficulty of royal works and thereby to admonish them to preserve and continue the dynasty; (3) to inform the people that General Yi Sŏng-gye founded the new kingdom because he had the mandate of Heaven and therefore did not usurp the throne; and (4) to institute the use of the compilation as court music in the ancestral temple and on official occasions and thereby to transmit it for myriads of years. There were a number of serious preparations at court and elsewhere for the compilation. On April 11, 1442, King Sejong ordered the governors of Kyŏngsang and Chŏlla provinces to gather from local elders facts and anecdotes concerning the exploits of T'aejo during his campaign against the Japanese pirates at Unbong

(1380). Further, on April 12, he ordered An Chi (d. 1464) and Nam Su-mun (1408-1442) to collect the tales of T'aejo's heroism which were not recorded in the official annals and to confirm the authenticity of those tales by checking with the surviving friends and followers of T'aejo. By this means both deeds preserved in the annals and popular traditions circulating among the people were assembled as materials for the compilation of this great eulogy-cycle. The *Yongbi ŏch'ŏn ka* is, therefore, a repository of fluid heroic tales and anecdotes connected with T'aejo and T'aejong, along with those concerning four royal ancestors of the founder. It also throws brilliant light, otherwise unavailable, on the Korean-Jurchen relationship of the same period (cantos 4, 53, 57, and 75).

The greatest importance of the *Yongbi ŏch'ŏn ka* lies in its philological aspect. The poems in this cycle are the first experimental use in verse of the new alphabet invented in 1443. The new phonetic letters were thus tested and revised before they were finally promulgated in 1446. It is therefore in the Korean verses of the *Yongbi ŏch'ŏn ka* that we can glimpse the *Urform* of the new alphabet. The texts still preserve such characteristics of the Late Middle Korean as the occurrence of letters that became obsolete before the eighteenth century, the use of initial consonantal clusters, the strong sense of vowel harmony, and the indication of tonemes. As the first document using the new alphabet, the *Yongbi ŏch'ŏn ka* furnishes us with the vocabulary and syntax of the Korean language in the fifteenth century and stands as one of the most important documents dating from the Middle Korean period.

The first canto, which is an introduction, clearly sets forth the theme of the book: praise of the four ancestors and the first and third kings of the Yi dynasty. The six dragons flying high in the land of the Eastern Sea are Mokcho (d.1274), Ikcho, Tojo (d. 1332), Hwanjo (d. 1360), T'aejo (1335-1392-1398), and T'aejong. The central part of the book covers cantos 3-124, subdivided into two sections. The first section, cantos 3-109, praises the cultural and military accomplishments of the six kings; the second section, cantos 110-124, consists of admonitions to future monarchs. Canto 125 is a conclusion. Each canto, except cantos 1, 2, and 125, consists of two poems, the first relating generally the great deeds of Chinese sovereigns and the second those of the Yi kings.[2] Both poems in cantos 110-124 deal with the Yi kings. In cantos 86-89, which are exceptions to the general scheme, both poems in each canto celebrate the deeds of Yi T'aejo. Cantos 108 and 109, the only cantos assigned to women, praise the heroic deeds of the consort of King Wen; Queen Sinhye of Wang Kŏn (877-918-943), the founder of Koryŏ; and Queen Wŏn'gyŏng (1365-1420), the consort of Yi T'aejong. The compilers assigned five cantos to Mokcho, eight cantos to Ikcho, four cantos to Tojo, six cantos to Hwanjo, eighty-one cantos to T'aejo, and twenty-three cantos to T'aejong.

We cannot compare the *Yongbi ŏch'ŏn ka* with the Western epic; the motives

[2]The first poem in canto 83 deals with the founder of Koryŏ.

of the compilers are too transparent. On the other hand, in literary art, in beauty and simplicity of language, in balanced and coherent structure, the anthology certainly occupies the highest position in the history of Yi dynasty poetry. There are moments of great dramatic intensity, and the poems are not without pathos and lyrical beauty (e.g., cantos 109 and 125). The *Yongbi ŏch'ŏn ka* mirrors the ideas not only of the new government, but also of the entire people. The compilers, as they state in the Preface, selected words and expressions from the popular language which were neither vulgar nor inadequate. Ideas of loyalty and nobility, of kingly virtue, of the foundation of a dynasty as the fruit of vast and difficult royal work, of "joy after sorrow" — all this is the kernel of the thinking of that time and culture. As the compilers state again, these poems "will be ineffaceable from the memory of man."

The *Wŏrin ch'ŏn'gang chigok* ("Songs of the Moon's Reflection on a Thousand Rivers"), composed by King Sejong, is another invaluable classic written in the new alphabet. Upon the death of Queen Sohŏn in 1446,[3] the king ordered his second son, Prince Suyang (later Sejo), to compile a life of Buddha. The prince gathered the existing materials on the subject and compiled the *Sŏkpo sangjŏl*, with emphasis on the eight aspects of the Buddha's life. The Preface is dated September 4, 1447; the book was published sometime later in the same year. The *Sŏkpo sangjŏl* is believed to have consisted of more than 200 sections, published in twenty-four volumes. Today only volumes 6, 9, 11, 13, and 19 are extant. After reading the melodic and simple prose of the *Sŏkpo sangjŏl,* the king was moved and composed the poems praising the life of Śākyamuni that are known under the title of *Wŏrin ch'ŏn'gang chigok*. These were completed probably in 1448 and were published about 1449. The number extant is 328 poems out of a total of 585, a figure established by recent scholarship. Later King Sejo (1417-1456-1468) published the *Sŏkpo sangjŏl* and *Wŏrin ch'ŏn'gang chigok* together under the title of *Wŏrin sŏkpo* in 1459. The *Wŏrin sŏkpo* originally consisted of more than twenty volumes, but today only volumes 1, 2, 7, 8, 9, 10, 13, 14, 17, 18, 21, and 23 are extant.

The form of the *Wŏrin ch'ŏn'gang chigok* is similar to that of the *Yongbi ŏch'ŏn ka*. Each canto consists generally of two poems, and the number of syllables in a poem fluctuates commonly between twenty-one and twenty-four. In style as well as in matter the *Wŏrin ch'ŏn'gang chigok* stands closer to the cult of devotional verse in Korea. The motive of this royal composition was both literary and devotional: the king's unending desire to experiment and disseminate the new alphabet, and his strong religious fervor to spread the wonderful law of Buddha among the people. The language is sublime and elegant, commensurate with the theme, and brocaded with rich imagery. It is more smooth and natural than that of the *Yongbi ŏch'ŏn ka* and is free from artificial parallelism and empty rhetoric. The section describing the birth of Siddhārtha,

_____

[3]The queen died April 19, 1446.

in particular, has Longinian sublimity in tone and expression. It is indeed un-usual for any sovereign to pour out his religious fervor and literary talent in such a voluminous and great work of art. It is no wonder, then, that literary historians should rank Sejong as the greatest poet-king of Korea.

Bibliography: the *Akchang*
A. *Yongbi ŏch'ŏn ka*

Cho Yun-je, *Chosŏn siga sagang* (1937), pp. 158-210.
_____, *Hanguk munhak sa* (1963), pp. 125-132.
Hŏ Ung, ed., *Yongbi ŏch'ŏn ka*, (1956).
Kim Sa-yŏp, *Yijo sidae ŭi kayo yŏn'gu* ("Studies in Yi Dynasty Poetry") (1956), pp. 15-227.
Kim Sŏng-ch'il, tr., *Yongbi ŏch'ŏn ka* (2 vols.; 1959).
Yi Sang-ch'un, *Chuhae Yongbi ŏch'ŏn ka* (1946).
. . .
Kang Sin-hang, *"Yongbi ŏch'ŏn ka* ŭi p'yŏnch'an kyŏngwi e taehayŏ" ("Circumstances of the Compilation of the *Yongbi ŏch'ŏn ka"), Mullidae hakpo*, VI/1 (1958), 147-151.
Kim Hyŏng-gyu, "Yongga Wŏrin e innŭn 'ni' e taehayŏ" ("On 'ni' in the *Yongbi ŏch'ŏn ka* and *Wŏrin ch'ŏngang chigok"), Ŏmun.* II/1 (1950), 9-13.
Kim Su-gyŏng, *"Yongbi ŏch'ŏn ka* sabip chaŭm ko" ("Consonantal Infixes in the *Yongbi ŏch'ŏn ka"), CH*, 15 (1947), 114-132.
Kim Yun-gyŏng, *"Yongbi ŏch'ŏn ka* e nat'anan yenmal ŭi pyŏnch'ŏn" ("Changes in the Meaning of Some Words in the *Yongbi ŏch'ŏn ka"), TH*, IV (1959), 205-231.
Pang Chong-hyŏn, *"Yongbi ŏch'ŏn ka* kanĝui"("Lectures on the *Yongbi ŏch'ŏn ka"), HG*, 100, 102, 103, 104, 105 (1947-1949).
Yi Hŭi-sŭng, "Sabyoŏ (ŭm) e taehayŏ" ("The Infixes in the *Hunmin chŏngŭm* and *Yongbi ŏch'ŏn ka"), STN*, II (1955), 45-61.
Yi Ki-mun, *"Yongbi ŏch'ŏn ka* kugŏ kasa ŭi chemunje" ("Problems in the Korean Verses of the *Yongbi ŏch'ŏn ka"), AY*, V/1 (1962), 87-128.

B. *Wŏrin ch'ŏngang chigok* and *Sŏkpo sangjŏl*

Hŏ Ung and Yi Kang-no, *Chuhae Wŏrin ch'ŏngang chigok* ("Annotated *Wŏrin ch'ŏn-gang chigok"),* Vol. I (1962).
Yi Tong-nim, *Wŏrin sŏkpo chebon ko* ("A Study of Different Editions of the *Wŏrin sŏkpo")* (n.d.).
_____, *Chuhae Sŏkpo sangjŏl* ("Annotated *Sŏkpo sangjŏl")* (1959).
Yŏnse University Far Eastern Institute, ed., *Wŏrin sŏkpo*, Vols. 9-10. (1956).
_____, *Wŏrin sŏkpo*, Vols. 7, 8, 17, 18 (1957).
Cho Mun-je, "Kyeryongsan Kapsa sojang *Wŏrin sŏkpo:* kwŏn isibil Ssanggyesa p'anmok e taehayŏ" (*"Wŏrin sŏkpo* Preserved in the Kap Temple on Mt. Kyeryong: On the Woodblocks of Volume 21 in the Ssanggye Temple"), *KK*, 20 (1959), 188-190.
Kang Sin-hang, "Yijoch'o pulgyŏng ŏnhae kyŏngwi e taehayŏ" ("On the Korean Trans-lation of Buddhist Scriptures in the Early Yi Dynasty"), *KY*, 1 (1957), 1-68.
Nam Kwang-u, *Kugŏhak nonmunjip* (1962), pp. 385-410.
Pak Pyŏng-ch'ae, *"Wŏrin ch'ŏngang chigok* ŭi p'yŏnch'an kyŏngwi e taehayŏ" ("The Circumstances Surrounding the Compilation of the *Wŏrin ch'ŏngang chigok"), Mulli nonjip*, VI (1962), 73-110.
Yi Tong-nim, *"Wŏrin sŏkpo* wa kwan'gye pulgyŏng ŭi koch'al" ("A Study of the *Wŏrin sŏkpo* and Related Buddhist Scriptures"), *PPN*, pp. 731-748.

V. The *Sijo*

The form of short lyric poem known as "sijo" existed at least 400 years before the name of its genre was invented by Yi Se-ch'un in the middle of the eighteenth century. Yi Se-ch'un, one of the most inventive musicians and singers of the day, composed a new tune that was known as a *sijŏl kajo* ("popular musical tune") and was a departure from the existing *kagok* tunes. The term *sijo* is a later abridgement of *sijŏl kajo*. Before being used to designate a definite poetic genre, it first came into being as a term for a new musical tune. The poetic form known today as *sijo* was formerly called by various names, *tan'ga* ("short lyric poem"), *sijo* or *sinbŏn, changdan'ga,* and *sinjo.* Soon the existing song words for the *kagok* tunes came to be sung to the new tune Yi had composed, and new poems were subsequently written directly for the *sijo* tune.

The origin of this form of short lyric verse, *sijo,* is still disputed among scholars. One theory attempts to find it in the *Saenaennorae* forms in Silla; another tries to find its origin in the Buddhistic poems imported from the Ming dynasty; a third conjectures that this was a form of poetry discovered in the process of translating Chinese poetry into Korean; a fourth says that it may be a modification of short-poem forms of the Koryŏ dynasty; a fifth traces its origin to the hymns chanted by shaman priests and priestesses. The *sijo* form is differentiated by its inner form — its attitude, emotional tone, and view of life — and by its audience.

Generally speaking, the *sijo* is a short, polished poem — more personal, specific, and local than the proverb — ending with a graceful, profound, and witty turn of thought. Yet the soul of the *sijo* is not wit, but sensibility. In Korea, the *sijo* was an art for the many, and every educated man and woman used this form for almost any purpose. Every topic, every mood, every style was possible. It was, as a Renaissance critic classified the epigram, "sweet, sour, bitter, and salt." A writer was not only familiar with its tradition and with its concentrated art, but was so deeply versed in it that he did not have to struggle to conform to its strict rules. In consequence, many *sijo* were composed extempore, ordinarily to be sung to a lute accompaniment. But the marvel is that they still show the marks of tradition and discipline, of grace and harmony. Thus the *sijo,* to the writers of the Yi dynasty, was an art in which words and music formed a single unit. A great body of the *sijo* was gathered in anthologies during the eighteenth and nineteenth centuries. The norm consists of a stanza of three lines with fourteen to sixteen syllables in a line, the total number of syllables never more than forty-five. Internally this triplet is again divided into three sections: beginning, middle, and end. Each line has generally four syllable groups, but internally it can be divided into two groups of several syllables. A pause, equivalent to a caesura, comes after the second group of syllables in each line. In other words, it is a poem consisting of a three-line stanza, four feet (better described as a "breath group") in a line, and three to four syllables in a foot. Thus the basic form is as follows:

First line   3 4 4 4/3
Second line 3 4 4 4/3
Third line   3 5 4 3

We note here the following characteristics:

1) In the first and second lines, each group can have three or four syllables, sometimes fluctuating between two and six syllables.
2) The first group in the third line has invariably three syllables.
3) The second group in the third line should never have fewer than five syllables.

We have seen, therefore, that the first, second, third, fourth and sixth groups have more freedom as to the number of syllables they can carry, but the fifth group is the key to the technique of the *sijo* and must have three and five syllables.

The form just described is known as *p'yŏng sijo* ("standard" or "common" *sijo*). The first variation of the standard form, *chunghyŏng* or *ŏt sijo,* has one or more syllables in one of the five groups except the fifth group. In the second variation, known as *changhyŏng* or *sasŏl sijo,* two of the five groups (except the fifth group) can be expanded, sometimes to several dozen syllables. The *sasŏl sijo* occupies an important place in the history not only of Korean poetry but also of Korean *Geistesgeschichte.* The birth of this form coincides with the time when the so-called "practical learning" was substituted for the stagnant Neo-Confucianist ideology and when the novel started to be written. This form scorned the traditional exclamation or scenery sketch and took as its favorite theme the diverse aspects of daily life of the common people. It also drew much of its vocabulary from the common speech; its tone became more and more realistic, and its expression bold and direct.

We can see that the *sijo* in its form has several characteristics in common with other forms of Korean poetry and that in *sijo,* as in other forms, it is the number of groups of syllables that determines the basis of its concentrated art. As several scholars suggest, we may conjecture that the norm of the *sijo* was already present in religious or shamanistic hymns or in folk songs, that it survived throughout the ages, and that the form in due time became detached from religious hymns or folk songs and gradually crystallized into its present state. In consequence, the evolution of this genre was a slow one. Its origin may lie in ancient times, but it only came to be considered as an independent genre sometime during the Koryŏ dynasty. We cannot, however, assume that this occurred in the beginning or middle of the Koryŏ dynasty. If so, there must have been a considerable body of works in this form. Unfortunately until 1446 the Koreans did not have their own system of writing, and the *sijo* that might have existed in Koryŏ times were not handed down to us. The ones which are known to us today had all been translated into Chinese before 1446 and were later retranslated into the new alphabet, or had been orally transmitted until the invention of the new letters in which eventually they were recorded. Thus, during the Koryŏ dynasty, historical sources record some ten *sijo* by as many different poets, and these were necessarily all from near the end of the dynasty. At the same time, historical records attribute several *sijo* to the Paekche dynasty and the early Koryŏ, but the uncertainty of this chronology makes impossible a serious consideration of them. They are suspect for the literary historian, but we are safe in considering the earliest examples attributed to U T'ak (1262-1342) to be the starting point.

The *sijo* written toward the end of Koryŏ and the beginning of Chosŏn were often occasional pieces. They were either retrospective or panegyric: retrospective ones written by the surviving retainers of Koryŏ (Kil Chae [1353-1419] and Wŏn Ch'ŏn-sŏk [fl. 1370-1395]) and panegyric ones by meritorious subjects of the new kingdom (Pyŏn Kye-ryang) upon the vastness of the royal works. Many political changes also inspired writers to lament disorder in the country (Sŏng Sam-mun, 1418-1456), and to display both their command of pathos and their versatility of style. On one occasion, a general sang of the victory of his army over the Jurchens (Kim Chong-sŏ, 1405-1453). Among the soldier-poets Yi Sun-sin (1545-1598), a famous admiral whose victories turned the tide of war during the Japanese invasion (1592-1598), left several *sijo* of high literary merit. On other occasions kings and subjects sang of constancy and loyalty (King Sŏngjong and Yu Ho-in [1445-1494], King Chungjong and Kim Ku [1488-1534], and King Myŏngjong and Song Sun [1493-1582]). The same period produced many social and political satires which were neither blunt nor unpolished, and were sufficiently brilliant and refined to be read as poetry.

In the sixteenth century, from the time of King Chungjong, scholar-poets came to be active on the literary scene. The first of these poets was Yi Hyŏn-bo (1467-1555), who rewrote a current *sijo* cycle of twelve poems into a cycle of nine poems (1548). The two most famous Neo-Confucianists, Yi Hwang (1502-1571) and Yi I (1536-1584), wrote similar *sijo* cycles in which they showed a keen appreciation of the beauties of nature. What they desired was to live in a hermitage among the mountains far from the din and bustle of the world. There were, however, two kinds of scholar-poets: those who had tried the official world and tasted bitter disappointment, and those aging government officials who intended to spend their later days in retirement. Their motives might be different, but they were one in their search for a quiet life among the settings of nature. When they met by the fountain or near the lake, they either devoted themselves to reading, or made friends with the morning flower or evening moon among the streams and stones. Thus their works were either learned and didactic, inculcating the teachings of ancient sages (e.g., Yi Hwang), or sentimental and escapist, singing of the hills and waters (e.g., Yi I). The influence of the scholar-poets on the academic world was not slight. Encouraged by their nature poetry and by their use of the *sijo* form instead of conventional Chinese verse-forms, students of Neo-Confucianism began to take a serious interest in this art.

The essence of the glorious tradition of the *sijo* was preserved and continued by Hwang Chin-i (fl. 1506-1544), the greatest Korean poetess of all periods. She was a famous *kisaeng* at Songdo (modern Kaesŏng), and her fame in poetry and music was widespread in the capital. She was a master technician and knew how to develop the chosen image on a dramatic plane. Her images were always simple and sensuous, generally drawn from nature, but they were always chosen for analogy and double vision. Not only is natural imagery used as a metaphor of the speaker's emotion; nature herself is personified and allegorized to produce many levels of meaning. From this kind of symbolism comes a unique intensity.

> Blue mountains speak of my desire,
> Green waters reflect my Lover's love:
> The mountains unchanging,
> The waters flowing by.
> Sometimes it seems the waters cannot forget me,
> They part in tears, regretting, running away.

Here allegory is tinged with metaphysical and even religious overtones. Hwang Chin-i's perception and intuition of the great theme of mutability and the relationship between transcendence and immanence is rendered into sensuous visual images. Here she approximates, *mutatis mutandis,* the technique of the English Metaphysical poets. Her poetry is characterized by a wealth of symbolism, a metrical orchestration, a harmonious order of words, and finally a mastery and flawless development of theme.

Chŏng Ch'ŏl (1536-1593) stands out from among a host of writers in the sixteenth century. He is more famous for his discursive poems than for his *sijo*; but he was not an ignoble writer in the *sijo* form. Among the seventy-nine poems contained in the *Songgang kasa* ("Pine River Anthology"), five poems (nos. 44, 45, 64, 70, and 77) are wrongly attributed to him. Unlike his *kasa* poems (see chap. vi) Chŏng's *sijo* drew much of their vocabulary from common words and phrases, digging deeply into native stores rather than taking inspiration from foreign sources. His *sijo* poems are simple in syntax and vocabulary, but he was subtle in weaving words together and relied for effect on a cunning juxtaposition which "gave back a familiar word as new."[1] He was skilled in the treatment of obvious themes, and in general, his poems are free from dense figures of speech or obscure allusions. The first sixteen poems (1580) in the *Songgang kasa* are finger-exercises showing his discipleship to the cult of moral verse of the Yi period. His favorite theme is his bitter resentment of court intrigue and the royal folly of which he was a victim. Following the tradition of the *Ch'u tz'u* poems,[2] the poet, despite the maltreatment he had suffered from the sovereign, still longs and searches for his "lord" (nos. 18, 19, 20, 23, 28, 29, 30, 32, 34, 60, 71, 74, and 78). Poem 42 is a vigorous poem containing a stern warning to the king not to succumb to slander. The poems in another group are allegorical or symbolic, and the south pole star (no. 33) and the crane (nos. 35 and 37) are compared to the speaker's state of mind.

> 33. Upon the familiar Sigyŏng Arbor,
>   The south pole star shines; even when
>   Mulberry gardens have changed into a sea
>   And everything has trembled and overturned—
>   The star shines the brighter;
>   Ah, it ignores the dark world.

> 35. O white crane that soars high
>   Beyond the clouds in the blue sky.
>   For whose sake do you alight?
>   Do you long for the human world?
>   Take wing, noble bird, fly away,
>   Until your long wings shed feathers.

> 37. You wheel around, noble bird,
>   Until you shed your white feathers.
>   And soaring high in the blue vault,
>   You speak in solemn syllables:
>   "I shall soar and soar again
>   Until I have glimpsed the cosmos."

The poet is like the south pole star or the crane up in the sky that scorns the dusty world below. In poem 48 the movement of sycophants and corrupt courtiers is compared with carpenters running about to no purpose with "ink-cup and measure." In a third group are strongly autobiographical poems that

---

[1]Horace, *Ars Poetica*, 46-48: "In verbis etiam tenuis cautusque serendis,/ Dixeris egregie notum si callida verbum/ Reddiderit iunctura novum."

[2]Often translated as the "Elegies of Ch'u," the *Ch'u tz'u* is an anthology of poems attributed to Ch'ü Yüan, a statesman of Ch'u under King Huai (r. 328-299 B.C.), along with a number of works by his disciples or later imitators. See Burton Watson, *Early Chinese Literature* (New York, 1962), pp. 231-254. For a complete translation of this anthology see David Hawkes, *Ch'u Tz'u: The Songs of the South* (Oxford, 1959).

deal with wine, the Black Lute,[3] and the hermit life. The poet's love of wine is well revealed in many poems (nos. 21, 22, 24, 25, 26, 50, 54, 56, and 58) in which he holds an imaginary dialogue with wine in the form of question and answer. Poems 36 and 65 deal with Chŏng's profound understanding of the techniques of the Black Lute.

> 36. The third string on the Black Lute
>   Softens and soothes my spirit.
>   I pluck the gallant note,
>   Play a pizzicato with vigor.
>   Don't feel sad, sombre string,
>   I shall return and pluck you shortly.

> 65. I pluck the second note on the third string
>   Of the Lute of the Black Crane.
>   The sound surges like a stream broken forth from the ice,
>   Rushing toward the sea.
>   Distant raindrops too play in concert;
>   They beat lightly on the lotus leaves.

He was not a love poet primarily, but poems 57, 66, 67, 75, and 79 demonstrate his skill in conventional love songs.

The perfection of the *sijo* form was attained in the seventeenth and eighteenth centuries. Scholar-poets again played an important role in bringing this form of verse close to the public. When scholars raised their goblets, they were either "romantic" or philosophical. In the bamboo groves they lay, perceiving the final harmony of the world and the mystery of all created things. Their topics were often traditional, and they repeated familiar themes and moods: angling under the moon, "plowing with the clouds," sensuous contemplation of nature, praise of wine, ecstasy of love, sorrow of parting, complaint of desertion, beauty of friendship, fear of death, simplicity of country life, evanescence of life, and the like. At times they also took inspiration from foreign writers, such as T'ao Ch'ien (365-427), Li Po (701-762), Tu Fu (713-770), and the Sung dynasty poets. Themes may have been conventional, but their treatment and technique vary with each poet.

The seventeenth century produced a number of first-class poets. Among them were Pak In-no (1561-1643), Cho Chon-sŏng (1554-1629), Yi Hang-bok (1556-1618), Kim Sang-yong (1561-1637), Kim Sang-hŏn (1570-1652), and Yi Myŏng-han (1595-1645); but the master during this century was without doubt Yun Sŏn-do (1587-1671), who was one of the most versatile and inventive of all *sijo* writers. His lyrics are diverse in mood and method, and his mature poems abound in exquisite felicities. His vocabulary is simple yet forceful, common yet noble, and his masterly choice of the right word is

---

[3]*Kŏmungo* ("Black Lute") or *Hyŏnhak kŭm* ("Lute of the Black Crane") is a six-stringed instrument, said to have been imported from Chin through Koguryŏ.

unparalleled. Graceful yet delicately varied rhythm was native with him, and every poem demonstrates new techniques and new tone. His poems number seventy-five altogether. Yun has been credited as a discoverer of the beauty of the Korean language. The hidden potentialities of the genre were thoroughly exploited by him, and certainly he brought not only progress, but perfection to the *sijo* art.

A group of six poems entitled *Kyŏnhoe yo* ("Expelling Gloom," 1618) was written by Yun in Kyŏngwŏn, during his first banishment. They are the earliest poems that we know of the poet, and have a tendency toward abstraction and the pathetic fallacy. Here the young poet expresses his pure longing for the king and for his parents, and declares that his sins were nothing but expressions of his loyalty and love. In "After the Rain" Yun echoes a famous Chinese poem, traditionally attributed to Ch'ü Yüan, in which a fisherman admonishes Ch'ü Yüan with the words: "When the Ts'ang-lang's waters are clear, I can wash my hat-strings in them: when the Ts'ang-lang's waters are muddy, I can wash my feet in them." Eighteen poems grouped under the heading "New Songs in the Mountain" (1642-1645) were written at the Grotto of Golden Chains. This group contains the immortal "Songs of Five Friends", addressed to water, stone, pine, bamboo, and the moon. Let me quote all six poems in the group, for they mark the highest achievement in the Korean language.

> How many friends have I? Count them:
> Water and stone, pine and bamboo —
> The rising moon on the east mountain,
> Welcome, it too is my friend.
> What need is there, I say,
> To have more friends than five?

> They say clouds are fine; I mean the color.
> But, alas, they often darken.
> They say winds are clear; I mean the sound.
> But, alas, they often cease to blow.
> It is only the *water,* then,
> That is perpetual and good.

> Why do flowers fade so soon
> Once they are in their glory?
> Why do grasses yellow so soon
> Once they have grown tall?
> Perhaps it is the *stone,* then,
> That is constant and good.

> Flowers bloom when it is warm;
> Leaves fall when days are cool.
> But, O *pine,* how is it
> That you scorn frost, ignore snow?

I know now your towering self,
Straight even among the Nine Springs.

You are not a tree, no,
Nor a plant, not even that.
Who let you shoot so straight; what
Makes you empty within?
You are green in all seasons,
Welcome, *bamboo,* my friend.

Small but floating high,
You shed light on all creation.
And what can match your brightness
In the coal dark of the night?
You look at me but with no words;
That's why, O *moon,* you are my friend.

Yun's "New Songs in the Mountain Continued" (eight poems altogether) contain "At the Beginning of the Feast" and "At the End of the Feast" (1645), consisting of two poems each. These were written with a clear didactic intent in mind and are admonitions to the king, but it is uncertain whether they are impromptu poems composed at an actual feast or simple admonitions. In the first poem, "a house" alludes to the ideal state, and "the straight tree" to benevolent government. "The work of the artisan" in the second line implies that the king should follow the way of the ancient sage-kings. In the second poem "wine" and "broth" allude to the virtues of the king, and "yeast" and "herbs" to the wise ministers who assist in state affairs. Another of the poems sings of moderation in pleasure. Perhaps the poet had in mind the 114th poem in the *Book of Songs,* in the first stanza of which the monitor says: "Do not be so riotous / As to forget your home. / Amuse yourselves, but no wildness! / Good men are always on their guard."[4]

Yun's *Ŏbu sasi sa* ("The Angler's Calendar," 1651), a *sijo* cycle consisting of forty poems, is his masterpiece. The poems cover the four seasons of the year and are products of his leisurely life at his favorite retreat, the Fairy Grotto; but they are, at the same time, a criticism of life and of his time. Here the peaceful pastoral life is strongly contrasted with the hypocrisies and injustices of court life. Structurally, the poems differ from the common *sijo* form, and the general pattern is as follows:

First line:	3	4	3	4
Refrain:	4	4		
Second line:	3	4	3	4
Refrain:	3	3		
Third line:	3	4	3	4

[4]Arthur Waley, tr., *The Book of Songs* (London, 1954), p. 199.

Therefore a pair of four syllables is added after the first line, and a refrain of three three-syllable onomatopoetic words after the second line, thus making the total number of syllables fifty-nine. The fortieth poem in this series has an unusual form in which the total number of syllables is seventy-two. The following are the first ten poems on spring from this famous cycle.

> The fog lifts in the stream before me
> And the sun lances the back hills.
> The night tide neaps, and now
> The high water rushes upon the shore.
> Heave away, ho, scull the boat,
> Distant hills and waters swell my heart.

> Welcoming day is fresh and fervent,
> Fishes leisurely float in the blue.
> Weigh anchor, friends, heave it up,
> Gulls appear, wing upon wing.
> Heave away, ho, I have a rod;
> Have you loaded a flagon of wine?

> A puff of east wind ruffles
> The surface of the stream into ripples.
> Hoist sail, friends, spread the sail,
> Let's go to West Lake by the East.
> Heave away, ho, scull the boat,
> Hills pass by, and more hills greet us.

> Is it a cuckoo that cries?
> Is it the willow that is blue?
> Several roofs in a far fishing village
> Swim in the dusk, magnificent.
> Boy, fetch an old net!
> Fishes are climbing against the stream.

> The sun's lanceheads are shining,
> Water is calm, calm as oil.
> Should we cast a net at all, friends,
> Should we drop a line on such a day?
> The poem of Ch'ü Yüan stirs my fancy;
> I have forgotten all about fishing.

> Let's return to our grass sill,
> Twilight trails in the pious west.
> Lower sail and scan the riverbank,
> Willows and flowers are supple and sweet,
> Who would envy three dukes?
> Who would now think of caps and gowns?

Let us tread on fragrant grasses
And pick orchids and irises.
Stopping the boat small as a leaf,
I ask what I have taken aboard.
Nothing except myself when I set sail,
When I row back, the moon is my tenant.

Drunk I will lie asleep,
And leave the boat only before the shoal.
Moor the boat, friends, Arcadia is near,
Crimson petals leap on the stream.
O sweet joy of the angler's life —
Can the dusty world last long?

Let's stop angling and salute
The moon framed in raspberry canes.
Drop anchor, friends, night settles,
The cuckoo too sings a sweet song.
The heart shouts its peak of joy,
I have lost my way in the dark.

Tomorrow, tomorrow, we have tomorrow,
A spring night will soon see the day.
Boat ashore and rod for a cane,
Let's find our brushwood door.
Spring stirs the joy in my veins.
O how many sweet days, sheer content!

A last group of three poems, entitled *Mongch'ŏn yo* ("The Disappointing Journey," 1652), was written when Yun entered the capital after seventeen years of absence and, owing to courtly intrigue, had to retire to his retreat after a month's stay. Here the "Jade Emperor" is King Hyojong (1619-1650-1659), and a "host of fairies" are Yun's opponents. In the last poem, he laments the absence of wise ministers who could repair the "pavilion of white jade" — that is, who could save the state from the evils of the times.

From the eighteenth century on, the *sijo* entered a new phase of development. This era corresponds to the period of the rise of the novel and of a middle class. In poetry it meant the retreat of the aristocracy who had dominated the literary scene for centuries, and the appearance of writers from the middle and lower classes. These new writers composed the *sijo* extempore, improvising freely to the existing tunes. Their language is simple and direct, and does not refrain from using rustic and unrefined vocabulary. Their tone is often hedonistic and their works are rich in realism and humor. Chu Ŭi-sik (1675-1720), Yi Chŏng-bo (1692-1766), Kim Yu-gi (fl. 1675-1700), Kim Ch'ŏn-t'aek (c. 1725-1766), Kim Su-jang (b. 1690), and Kim U-gyu (c. 1740) are some of the important poets of this period. The famous anthologists Kim Ch'ŏn-t'aek and

Kim Su-jang merit special mention not only as *sijo* poets, but as important musicians of the day. They stressed the musical quality of the *sijo*, composed both words and tunes, and sang their works to musical accompaniment before large audiences. Two poets who emerged toward the end of the nineteenth century, Pak Hyo-gwan (fl. 1850) and An Min-yŏng (c. 1870), have a singular place in the history of the *sijo*. They gave, so to speak, the final touch to this form of verse before the fall of the Yi dynasty.

The *sijo* is still the favorite classical form of verse, and the twentieth century has produced many first-class poets in this genre. They have written individual *sijo* and *sijo* cycles as well as the *sasŏl sijo*. It is interesting to note that the better poets have excelled in *sijo* cycles. The classical form is kept in every respect except the number of lines. The traditional *sijo* is, as we have seen, a poem of three lines consisting of six syllable groups (or twelve when subdivided). Modern poets, influenced by Western versification, have often extended the number of lines to five or as many as ten lines; the number of syllables is still forty-five, as in the traditional *sijo*. The first modern *sijo* cycle of importance was produced in 1926 by the late Ch'oe Nam-sŏn (1890-1957). In or about 1925. Yi Kwang-su (b. 1892) also wrote many cycles. Both in output and quality, Chŏng In-bo (b. 1892), Yi Pyŏng-gi (b. 1892), Yi Ŭn-sang (b. 1903), and Kim Sang-ok (b. 1915) should be mentioned. But the *sijo* is no more sung to musical accompaniment; it is generally meant to be read.

Bibliography: the *Sijo*

Cho Yun-je, *Chosŏn siga sagang* (1937), pp. 115-129, 210-223, 247-276, 296-414.
——————————, *Chosŏn siga ŭi yŏn'gu* (1948), pp. 131-200.
——————————, *Hanguk munhak sa* (1963), pp. 94-102, 141-147, 160-168, 176-184, 208-235, 350-378.
——————————, *Kungmunhak kaesŏl* (1960), pp. 109-115.
Chŏng Pyŏng-uk, *Kungmunhak san'go* (1960), pp. 160-168, 190-211.
Lee, Peter H., "Introduction to the *Sijo*: the Epigram," *East and West,* VII, No. 1 (Rome, 1956), 61-66.
. . .
An Cha-san, *Sijo sihak* ("Poetics of *Sijo*") (1949).
Ch'oe Nam-sŏn, *Sijo yuch'wi* ("Anthology of *Sijo*") (1929).
Chŏng Ch'ŏl, *Songgang kasa,* ed. Pak Sŏng-ŭi (1956).
Chŏng Chu-dong and Yu Ch'ang-sik, *Chinbon Ch'ŏnggu yŏngŏn chusŏk* ("Annotated *Ch'ŏnggu yŏngŏn*") (1957).
Kim Su-jang, *Haedong kayo,* ed. Kim Sam-bul (1950).
Maema Kyōsaku, ed., *Kyoju kagok chip* ("Annotated Anthology of Korean Verse") (1951).
Pak Hyo-gwan and An Min-yŏng, *Kagok wŏllyu* (1952).
Songŏm hagin, ed., *Sijo charyo chipsŏng* ("Source Materials for *Sijo*") (n.d.).
Yi Chae-su, *Yun Kosan yŏn'gu* ("A Study of Yun Kosan") (1955).
Yi Ch'ang-bae, *Chŭngbo kayo chipsŏng* ("A Collection of Korean Songs") (1959).
Yi Chu-hwan, *Kogŭm sijo sŏn* ("A Selection of *Sijo,* Ancient and Modern") (1958).

Yi Nŭng-u, *Yijo sijo sa* ("History of Yi Dynasty *Sijo*") (1956).
Yi Pyŏng-gi, *Sijo ŭi kaesŏl kwa ch'angjak* ("Outline and Technique of *Sijo*") (1957).
Yi T'ae-gŭk, *Kungmin sasang kwa sijo munhak* ("Korean Spirit and *Sijo* Literature'.')
    (1955).
Yu Ch'ang-don, *Ko sijo e nat'anan sŏnin tŭrŭi saenghwal inyŏm* ("Korean Modes of
    Life as Revealed in Classical *Sijo*") (1952).
Yun Sŏn-do, *Kosan siga,* ed. Pak Sŏng-ŭi. 1956.

. . .

Chang Sa-hun, "*Kurach'ŏlsagŭm po* ŭi haedok kwa hyŏnhaeng p'yŏngsijo ŭi chemunje"
    ("Deciphering of the *Kurach'ŏlsagŭm* Score and the Problems of Current *Sijo*"),
    AY, I/2 (1958), 107-127.
_____, "*Maehwajŏm* changdan ko" ("The Rhythm of *Maehwajŏm*"), *YHS,*
    pp. 583-611.
Ha Sŏng-nyŏn, "*Sijo* sang e nat'anan inmul ko" ("On the Characters Appearing in
    Sijo"), *KKY,* 2 (1958), 73-94.
Kim Kŭn-su, "Sijo non" ("On *Sijo*"), *Wŏndae hakpo,* 1 (1956), 58-83.
Kim Sang-sŏn, "Ko sijo chongjang yŏn'gu" ("A Study of the Third Line of *Sijo*"), *CTN,*
    VII (1962), 133-155.
Ku Cha-gyun, "Nogye ŭi kasa wa sijo ŭi kyoju" ("The *Kasa* and *Sijo* of Pak In-no,
    with Annotations"), in *Fiftieth Anniversary Volume of Korea University* (1955), pp.
    555-596.
Min Yŏng-bo, "Hyangga munhak kwa sijo hyŏngsŏng e taehan yŏksajŏk yŏn'gu" ("A
    Historical Study of *Hyangga* and Its Relation to the Rise of the *Sijo*"), *CTN,* VII
    (1962), 105-132.
Pak Chun-gyu, "Yijo wangson tŭrŭi sijo munhak yŏn'gu" ("*Sijo* by Members of the Yi
    Royal Family"), *Chŏnnam University Kungmunhak po,* 3 (1962), 95-188.
Sim Chae-wan, "*Pyŏngwa kagok chip* ŭi yŏn'gu" ("A Study of the *Pyŏngwa kagok
    chip*"), in *Tenth Anniversary Volume of Ch'ŏnggu University* (1958), pp. 139-202.
_____, "*Kŭmok ch'ongbu* (*Chuong manp'il*) yŏn'gu" ("A Study of the
    Kŭmok ch'ongbu"), *CGTN,* IV (1961), 37-61.
Sŏk Yŏng-su, "Yijo yŏryu sijo chakp'um non" ("On the *Sijo* of Women Poets during the
    Yi Dynasty"), *KKY,* 2 (1958), 173-199.
Tada Masatomo, "*Ch'ŏnggu yŏngŏn* to *Kagok wŏllyu*" ("*Ch'ŏnggu yŏngŏn* and *Kagok
    wŏllyu*"), *Oda sensei shōju kinen Chosŏn ronshū* (1934), pp. 545-598.
Yi Chong-ch'ul, "Sijo munhak ŭi sidaejŏk sŏngkyŏk" ("The Contemporary Features of
    Sijo Literature"), *Tongguk taehak,* 1 (1955), 166-181.
Yi Nŭng-u, "Yijo ŭi hŭisiga" ("The Love Theme in the Popular *Sijo* of the Yi Dynas-
    ty"), *HM,* II/12 (1956), 219-227; III/1 (1957), 81-86; III/2, 108-115; III/3, 256-262.
Yi Nŭng-u, "Yijo siga mood ŭi saekch'ul" ("An Inquiry into the Poetic Moods of the
    Yi Dynasty"), *YHS,* pp. 409-430.
Yi T'ae-gŭk, "Sijo ŭi yŏnhyŏngch'e mit kisa hyŏngsik" ("The Linking Style and Stanzaic
    Forms of *Sijo*"), *YHS,* pp. 531-555.
Yu Ch'ang-sŏn, "Nongam ŭi sigagwan" ("The View of Poetry of Nongam [Yi Hyŏn-
    bo]"), *Ŏmunhak,* 4 (1959), 60-76.

Translations

Lee, Peter H., *Kranich am Meer,* pp. 34-90.

———————, "The Life and Poetry of Yun Sŏn-do, the Greatest Poet in the *Sijo* Form," *Monumenta Serica,* XXI (Nagoya, 1962).

———————, "The *Songgang kasa* of Chŏng Ch'ŏl," *T'oung Pao,* XLIX (1961), 149-193.

———————, *Anthology of Korean Poetry,* pp. 63-67, 71-73, 75-92, 106-108, 110-111, 120-149, 153-158.

VI. The *Kasa*

The *kasa* can best be defined as a new form of verse originating as song words written to prevailing *kasa* tunes. Such tunes are numerous both in number and kind, and performance of a *kasa* poem to such tunes is extremely complicated. The *kasa* poem, sung by both men and women, is divided into five sections, with a set number of drum beats, hand clappings, and elaborate regulations governing the phrasings. The musical aspect of the *kasa* properly belongs to the domain of music; we are concerned here with its literary aspects, the texts of the poems written for *kasa* tunes. Since song words thus written had to conform closely to the existing tunes, in the process of "fitting words to a tune" a pattern of composition was established for the poet, and this pattern was soon regarded as a definite verse form. Today the *kasa* are chiefly known by the titles of the song words written for the tunes rather than by the names of the tunes themselves.

As a new genre of vernacular verse, the *kasa* appeared first toward the middle of the fifteenth century. It is regarded as the modified form of the long poems of Koryŏ, and some scholars maintain that the norm of this form was already visible in the poems written in the twelfth century and thereafter.[1] What differentiates it from the *changga* is that it has no stanzaic division, but continues on like a chain, and has a tendency toward description and exposition rather than subjective lyricism. The earlier examples of this kind are, however, rich in subjective lyricism, sometimes even in the outburst of emotion; the latter examples tend to be more realistic and, often, "journalistic." The *kasa* has such characteristics as the use of accentuation and rhythm, of the caesure, and of balanced parallel phrases, verbal and grammatical parallelism in particular. This is why one theory attempts to compare it with the *fu* (prose poetry). The norm of this new genre is a group of two four-syllable words which forms a single unit and is repeated in parallel form. The *kasa* varies in length from a poem longer than the *changga* of Koryŏ to several thousand lines.

The earliest extant poem of this type is the *Sangch'un kok* ("Hymn to the Spring," c. 1455-1480), by Chŏng Kŭg-in (1401-1481). This poem, forty lines

---

[1]Strictly speaking, however, the *kasa* is a development from the second variant form of the *kyŏnggi*-style verse as it passed through the transitional period of the *akchang* form. The *kasa*, therefore, inherited from these two forms of verse their two special characteristics—from the first its aristocratic and escapist nature and from the second its typically Confucian element.

altogether, sings of the beauty of pastoral life and is divided into four parts: introduction, spring scenery, the poet's pleasure among hills and waters, and a conclusion. This form of verse was perfected in the end of the sixteenth and the first two quarters of the seventeenth century by Chŏng Ch'ŏl, Hŏ Nan-sŏrhŏn (1563–1589), and Pak In-no (1561-1643). Chŏng left five *kasa,* and his contemporaries ranked him as first among the poets of the Yi dynasty. The first *kasa,* the *Kwandong pyŏlgok* ("The Wanderings," 1580), is a poem of 146 lines, divided into four parts, describing the eight famous scenes in the Diamond Mountains. The poet begins with his appointment as governor of Kangwŏn province and an account of his journey from Seoul to the entrance of the Inner Diamond Mountains. He fondly describes waterfalls, ravines, high peaks, famous temples, pavilions, and arbors in brilliant and majestic passages; the poem ends with a dream in which the poet holds an imaginary dialogue with a fairy. The *Sa miin kok* ("Hymn of Constancy," c. 1585-1587) and *Sok miin kok* ("Another Hymn of Constancy," c. 1585-1587) are allegorical poems in the *Li sao* tradition. They were written when the poet, because of factional strife, had to retire from the court and spend several years in country villages. In both poems he compares his constancy to King Sŏnjo (1552-1568-1608) to that of a distant wife longing for her husband. The first poem (sixty-three lines) is a monologue; the second (forty-eight lines) is a dialogue held by two court ladies. After a moving description of the miseries of the deserted wife, the poems end with her strong desire for transformation — in the first poem into a butterfly and the second into rain. The latter is generally preferred over the former for its sustained tone and beauty of diction. The following is a complete translation of the latter poem, using the text found in the Sŏngju edition of the *Songgang kasa.*

> "Lady, whose face I know, lady
> walking alone, tell me,
> why did you leave the royal palace,
> whom are you seeking as the sun goes down?"
> "Hear then my story.
>   My face and ways
> do not deserve his royal love, I know;
> yet when he sees, he deigns to recognize me,
> smiles with the same smile,
> welcomes me as of old.
> I cannot believe him changed.
> I lie and think, sit and measure,
> my sins heap up like mountains.
> I do not quarrel with Heaven or with men.
> Untie this sadness, undo this sorrow?
> No, it seems it is my ordained fate."

"Don't fret, my dear. There's something
eating *his* heart out, too.
I've served him, I know him.
                              He has had
little enough of peace these days, God knows.
Spring cold and summer heat,
long autumn and rueful winter days,
how did he spend them? Who served him?
Morning gruel and daily rice,
did he get enough?
Has he slept well, think you,
these long nights?"

"Ah, I want his news — but day is gone.
Would someone come tomorrow — restless thought!
Where shall I go, led or pushed?
                              The clouds
gather on solemn peaks, a mist
bewraps the world.
                      How then, lady,
can I see the brightness,
the brightness of sun and moon?
What's there — within a foot, within an inch?
A thousand miles is far, so far. . . . I'll go
down to the sea and wait a boat.
O, winds and waves are furious — I'm stunned —
the boatman's gone — only the empty ship —

Now darkness
creeps under the eaves of a hut. For whom
does that lamp burn on the wall there?
Up hill and down I go, or pace the shore.
At last my prayer is answered, and I see
Milord in dreams.
                      But time
has stolen away his jade face.
                              I want
to tell him all, all, to my heart's content,
but tears choke me, words stick in my throat.
I cannot speak my love or melt my grief.
A cock crows. Everything
was a mocking dream.
I open the window; only the shadows hover.
O, to be the moon and shine on his window."

"Lady, the moon, say you?
Rather a weeping rain!"

The *Sŏngsan pyŏlgok* ("Little Odes of Mount Star," c. 1585-1587) was
written by Chŏng to praise the elegant life of Kim Sŏng-wŏn centering around
the Sŏha Hall and Sigyŏng Arbor below Mount Star in South Chŏlla province.
I shall quote this poem in full, because it is one of the finest *kasa* poems dating
from the Yi dynasty, despite numerous learned allusions to both Chinese and
Korean poetry and personalities.

An unknown guest in passing
stopped on Mount Star and said:
"Listen, Master of the Sŏha Hall,
despite the many pleasures life held,
why did you prefer to them all
this mountain, this water?
What made you choose
the solitude of hills and streams?"

i

Sweeping away the pine needles,
setting a cushion on a bamboo couch
I casually climb into the seat
and view the Four Corners.
Floating clouds come and go
over the Sŏsŏk Terrace;
their flying motion and gentle gestures
resemble the mind and courtesy
of the noble Master of Sŏha.
The fresh stream, gold and silver,
flows past the Arbor;
as if the Weaver[2] Star had come to earth
the water rushes in endless patterns,
like cloud brocade, scissored and spread before us.
In the city, without a calendar who would know
the year's cycle? But here
every subtle change of the seasons
unrolls like a screen before us.
This is truly the land of the Immortals.

[2]The star Vega in the constellation of Lyra. These two lines allude to the beauty of the stream.

ii

Sun at the window caresses the plum tree;
the fragrance of blossoms wakes me.
Who says there is nothing
to keep an old hermit busy?
I sow melon, tend them, support them;
when the rain nurtures the young plants,
I think of the old tale of the Blue Gate.[3]
In straw sandals, with a bamboo cane,
I follow the plum-snowed causeway
over to Pangch'o Islet.
As I stroll by the West Brook
the stone screen accompanies me
in the water mirror, painted there, as if polished.
Where is Arcadia? Wu-ling is here.

iii

The casual south wind
disperses the tree shade, makes way
for a faithful cuckoo—where has he flown from?
I wake from a doze
on the pillow of ancient worthies
and see the reflected balcony floating
among the clouds in the lake.
With my arrowroot hat aslant
and my smock tucked into my belt,
I go nearer, and watch the drunken fishes
after the rainy night.
Here and there, red and white lotus:
their fragrance rises
into the windless sky
and passes over the hills.
As though I had met with Chou Tun-yi[4] and supped
on the Ultimate Secret—
or as if a faery had shown me the Jade Letters[5]—

---

[3]The Blue Gate is the southeast gate of Ch'ang-an. In the time of Ch'in, Shao P'ing was enfeoffed as the Marquis of Tung-ling. But when the Han destroyed the Ch'in he had to abandon his post and live by raising melons. The melons he raised were called either Tung-ling or Ch'ing-men melons.

[4]Chou Tun-yi (1017-1073), one of the great Sung philosophers, the author of the *Diagram of the Supreme Ultimate Explained.*

[5]A fairy elucidated the Canon of Jade, supposed to be written by the legendary Yellow Emperor. See *Wu-Yüeh ch'un-ch'iu* (*Ssu-pu pei-yao* ed.) VI, 1b-2a.

I glance toward Noja Rock by Chami shore,
letting a tall pine screen the sun,
sitting at ease on the stone path.

iv

In the bitter world of man it is June,
month of humid exhausting heat;
here in Elysium the air has the feel
of autumn, zestful and light.
A duck afloat on the stream moves in
to the white sand bar,
makes friends with the gulls.
Free and leisurely, it resembles
our host, the noble Master of Sŏha.

v

At the fourth watch the moon rises,
cold, over the paulownia trees.
Thousand cliffs, ten thousand ravines —
could they be brighter by daylight?
Who moved the Palace of Crystal from Huchou?[6]
Did I cross the Milky Way?
Have I reached the Moon Palace?
Setting out from the twin pines,
I let the boat drift downstream
passing the floating duckweed.
My friend, when did we reach
the cataract before Hwanbyŏk Hall?
Cowherds in the riverside pastures
were joyfully playing their pipes in the sunset light.
Do not awaken the sleeping dragon,
do not let cranes abandon their nests and take wing
into the smoky twilight.
Su Shih in his poem on Red Cliff[7]
praises the seventh moon above all;
but let us not underestimate
the August moon.

[6]Cannot locate this palace.

[7]Su Shih (1036-1101) says, in his preface to the *Red Cliff*, that it was written in the seventh moon. See Cyril Drummond le Gros Clark, *The Prose-Poetry of Su Tung-P'o* (Shanghai, 1935), p. 126: "In the autumn of the year Jen-hsü, when the seventh moon was on the wane, I, Su, was drifting with friends in a boat below the Red Cliff."

When the clouds part and water grows still,
the rising moon anchors herself in a pine branch.
They say Li Po drowned because of her.

vi

North winds sweep away
the heaped leaves on the wild mountains,
marshal the clouds, attack us with snow.
The Creator, He who loves
to fashion the things of nature,
makes snowflowers of white jade, devises
myriad new forms for the forests.
The foreshore freezes over, dazzles the eye.
Over the one-logged bridge
goes an old priest, a stick on his shoulder,
head on one side, sadly.
Where do you head for, friend? What temple
is richer in beauty than what you see
here in this world of the moon,
Mount Star in a fresh snowfall?

vii

Alone in the deep mountain
with no friend but the classics, pile on pile,
I think of the men of all times:
many were sages, many were heroes.
Heavenly intention goes into the making of men.
Yet fortunes rise and fall, and what is unknowable
seems to be chance. And sadness is deep.
Why did Hsü Yu on Mount Chi
cleanse his innocent ears?[8]

viii

The mind of the Master of Sŏha Hall
smiles like his face;
his friendship is new and fresh each day.
Let us not think of worldly affairs.

[8]Hsü Yu was a princely man in the time of the Emperor Yao. Knowing of his virtue and integrity, the Emperor suggested to him the possibility of leaving him the throne. Hsü Yu was too pure a man to listen to such an offer and went to the river to cleanse his ears. *Kao-shih chuan (Ssu-pu pei-yao* ed.), I, 2b-3a.

The wine brewed yesterday must be ready;
Let's drink, passing the cup back and forth,
pouring more wine till we are tired of it.
Then our hearts will be open, the net
of sorrow unraveled to nothing.
String the black lute and sing,
Who is host, who is guest?
The flying crane is the true Immortal
I met once in the Moon Palace.
The guest addresses the host with a word:
"You, sir, you alone are immortal."

His last poem, *Changjinju sa* ("A Time to Drink"), is Anacreontic, stressing Epicureanism and the emptiness of life without wine.

The *kasa* found its greatest poetess in Hŏ Nansŏrhŏn, sister of Hŏ Kyun, the author of the *Hong Kiltong chŏn* (see chap. viii). She left two poems, the *Pongsŏnhwa* ("Balsam,") and *Kyuwŏn ka* ("A Woman's Sorrow"). The former evokes in delicate and graceful language the beauty of the balsam, which is the favorite summer flower among young girls in Korea, who have their fingers dyed with balsam pounded in alum. The poem suggests, at the end, the fleetingness of the seasons and of human affairs, contrasting that with the permanence of the world of art. The *Kyuwŏn ka* is a dramatic narrative in which a lost lover reveals her miseries and longings in most vivid and convincing language. The tone and mood of the poem is set by the opening: "Yesterday I fancied I was young; / But already, alas, I am aging." The beauties and wonders of nature only worsen her sorrow and cause her to recall her happy childhood and girlhood. She finally takes out a green lute and plays a song of Blue Lotus, but her room is empty except for the lotus-brocaded curtains. The poem ends with the lines: "Think, love, you caused me this grief; / I know not whether I shall live or die."

After an unproductive period in the sixteenth century, the *kasa* found another poet in Pak In-no (1561-1643), the master of this form in the seventeenth century. Between 1598 and 1636 Pak produced seven major *kasa,* in quantity certainly unsurpassed, and in quality next only to those of Chŏng Ch'ŏl. He developed a style of his own which combines learnedness and lyricism. An ordered structure, virtuoso techniques, and rich vocabulary are some of the features of his works. The first poem, the *T'aep'yŏng sa* ("Song of Peace," 1598), was written during the Japanese invasion when the poet fought in the navy at Pusan. The battle was successful for the defenders, and the Japanese army was destroyed overnight. The poet returned to headquarters after ten days and, in recognition of the service rendered by the navy, composed this poem which praised the seamen. The poem begins with the confusion caused by the unexpected invasion of the Japanese, proceeds to praise the desperate fight and subsequent victory won by the allied armies of Ming and Korea, describes the joy of victorious homecoming and ends with a prayer to heaven and earth "That there be no more war, myriads of years, / That people sing in the field and by the well, / That they strike drums on the fertile soil, / That we always have a beloved king above us, / And that He and we share the joy of peace." Like the *T'aep'yŏng sa,* his *Sŏnsangt'an* ("Lament on the Water," 1605) took inspiration from the Japanese invasion. The poem digresses for several lines on the origin of ships. The poet holds the Yellow Emperor, the First Emperor, and Hsü Shih responsible for this invention which is now causing Korea much trouble, but soon returns to a description of his determined loyalty at the moment of national crisis. The poem ends with a prayer that the invaders will soon surrender and peace reign again; only then can he enjoy again the autumn moon and the spring breeze, rowing on moving waters. The *Saje kok* ("Song of the Sedge Bank," 1611) was written on the occasion of his visit to the summer resort of Yi Tŏk-hyŏng (1561-1613) at Saje ("Sedge Bank"), five leagues east of the Yongjin River. The poem describes the beautiful spots in Saje and Yi's idle life in that setting. When asked by the host about his life, the poet composed his famous *Nuhang sa* ("In Praise of Poverty"), a *kasa* which asserts the joy and contentment of a life of poverty and declares that the virtue of a gentleman is "to be poor and yet not resent his poverty" *(Analects,* XIV, 11).

The *Tongnaktang* ("The Hall of Solitary Bliss") was written by Pak on the occasion of his visit to the Tongnak Hall, a retreat of Yi Ŏn-jŏk (1491-1553), his former teacher, at Mount Jade in Kyŏngju. The poem praises the scenic beauty surrounding this hall, and reveals the poet's deep admiration for his teacher and recalls many memories. The *Yŏngnam ka* ("Song of the South," 1635) was written to praise Yi Kŭn-wŏn's good administration as governor of Kyŏngsang province. The *Nogye ka* ("Song of the Reedy Stream," 1636) deals with the scenic beauty of the Reedy Stream, a retreat of the poet, and describes his idyllic life.

In the times of Kings Yŏngjo and Chŏngjo (1725-1800) the *kasa* became predominantly a popular form of poetry among women and common folk. This change was partly owing to the rise of the novel about the same time and the decline of verse genres. The *kasa* occupied, as it were, a middle position between prose and verse, and the rise of prose and of the middle class brought about changes in the inner form of the *kasa,* its subject matter, its audience, and its tone. Whereas the previous *kasa* dealt chiefly with elegant pleasures among nature, the beauties of the four seasons, the praise of civilization, and the like, the subject matter of the new *kasa* was daily life itself, life of both men and women of the middle and lower classes. The new poets and poetesses rejected the empty and idealistic world which the poet-philosopher or scholar-statesman had once created; they relied solely on colloquial diction and conversational rhythm for effect and welded written and spoken language into one.

One feature of this period is that the *kasa* was mostly developed by women, particularly in the southeastern part of the peninsula. These women authors considered the study of the *kasa* the most important part of their education, and each woman, so we are told, knew by heart both the texts and tunes of several dozens of poems. Many *kasa* were composed extempore either to teach their friends and children or to entertain themselves and their friends with songs. Thus the *kasa* spread rapidly from the eighteenth century on, and the number of anonymous works dating from that period attests to the popularity of this genre at that time.

The *kasa* of definite authorship dating from the middle of the eighteenth century are mostly travel diaries. The *Iltong changyu ka* ("Song of a Journey to Japan," 1764), consisting of more than 4,000 lines, is a travel description by Kim In-gyŏm, who accompanied the Korean envoy to Edo (modern Tokyo). The journey started on September 9, 1763 and ended on August 5, 1764. The poem depicts in smooth and rhythmic language Kim's journey from Seoul to Pusan, the voyage from Pusan to Tsushima, his arrival in Edo, and his meeting with the Japanese men of letters. Upon his return to Seoul, Kim reported to the throne that he had composed several thousands of impromptu poems which he had distributed to the Japanese on their request as farewell gifts.

There are two verse records of travel to Peking, one anonymous (1798) and another (1866) by Hong Sun-hak. The latter is a long poem of 1,962 lines, covering the period of his departure from and return to Seoul (May 22 to September 23, 1866). The section on his meeting with the Chinese literati is of special interest.

The *Hanyang ka* ("Song of Seoul," 1844) is anonymous and consists of 812 lines. The poem, a eulogy on the institutions of the Yi dynasty, opens with the description of the beauty of the capital and then praises in succession the geographical features of Seoul, its palaces and pavilions, its offices and bureaus, its markets and merchants, and the manners and customs of the courtiers. It also has a vivid description of the scene of a civil service examination.

The *Pukch'ŏn ka* ("Song of a Northern Exile"), consisting of 607 lines, is by Kim Chin-hyŏng (b. 1801), Fifth Counselor in the Office of Special Counsellors. Kim was banished to Myŏngch'ŏn in the seventh moon of 1853, and the poem covers the period from his trip to Myŏngch'ŏn until his return to his birthplace, Andong, after the expiration of the term of banishment. The governor of Myŏngch'ŏn was a benevolent and broad-minded man and granted Kim maximum freedom. Kim was allowed not only to read and to teach children of the place, but also to explore the beauties of Mount Ch'ilbo, the famous beauty spot in Myŏngch'ŏn. There he met a *kisaeng,* Kun San-wŏl, who relieved his loneliness in exile. When released and returned to Andong, he could not bear to sever his ties with Kun San-wŏl, and the poem reaches its climax in the description of his intense love for his companion. Another poem of this type worthy of mention is the *Kwandong changyu ka* ("Song of the Diamond Mountains"), consisting of more than 700 lines. Like the *Kwandong pyŏlgok* of Chŏng Ch'ŏl, the subject matter of this poem is the Diamond Mountains.

We have discussed poems of definite date and authorship; but there are volumes of anonymous poems, among which the *Ch'unmyŏn kok* ("Spring Sleep," c. 1725) and *Kwandŭng ka* ("Song of the Lantern Feast," c. 1725) are outstanding examples. Only the first five sections of the *Kwandŭng ka* are preserved:

> On the day of the first full moon,
> The children play, enjoying the moon,
> They play, stamping on the bridge.[9]
> But where is he, ah, where is my Love?
> Alas, he is not on the bridge.
>
> On the day of the Clear and Bright,
> The lusty sap stirs the trees;
> Young buds spring among the grass;
> Everything grows in harmony—
> But where is he, ah, where is my Love?
> He knows not, alas, that spring is here.
>
> On the third day of the third moon,
> Swallows come, come from the south;
> And the wild geese from the Hsiao and Hsiang,
> They say they must bid us farewell.
> Plum and peach trees are in bloom,
> Apricot petals fall on the grass,
> They are scattered, whispering and falling.
> But where is he, ah, where is my Love?
> He knows not this is the season of flowers.
>
> On the eighth day of the fourth moon
> I climb the terrace to see the lanterns,
> Lit at sundown, far and near.
> Fish lanterns and dragon lanterns,
> Phoenix lanterns and crane lanterns,
> A heron and the southern star;
> Fairy lanterns and drum lanterns,
> Watermelon and garlic lanterns,
> A fairy messenger in the lotus,

[9]The people in Seoul, having heard the evening bell in the Chongno Square on the fifteenth day of the first moon, would leave off whatever they were doing and go to the bridges in the capital and stamp on them. This was supposed to prevent a sickness of the feet.

A celestial nymph on a fabulous bird,
Ship lanterns and house lanterns,
Egg lanterns and bottle lanterns,
Mask-play lanterns and shadow lanterns,
Closet, sedan, and rail lanterns,
A masked hero riding a lion,
Straw puppets on wolves and tigers —
And the sun lanterns and moon lanterns
Shine on the lanterns that roll on the ground,
And beyond the arch of the plough lanterns
Rises the moon over East Mountain,
And below, windows are lit here and there.
But where is he, ah, where is my Love?
He knows not how the lanterns shine.

On the fifth day of the fifth moon,
Other folks' children install a swing.
Gaily they play on the swings, up and down,
Hurtling downwards, zooming upwards —
But where is he, ah, where is my Love?
He knows not it is the season of swings.

This form of verse was no longer popular after the fall of the Yi dynasty.

Bibliography: *The Kasa*

Chang Tŏk-sun, *Kungmunhak t'ongnon* ("Outline of Korean Literature," 1960), pp. 351-384.
Cho Yun-je, *Chosŏn siga sagang* (1937), pp. 223-227, 232-247, 261-267, 277-295.
_____, *Chosŏn siga ŭi yŏn'gu* (1948), pp. 116-130.
_____, *Hanguk munhak sa* (1963), pp. 169-176, 235-241, 332-350.
_____, *Kungmunhak kaesŏl* (1960), pp. 137-151.

Kim Sa-yŏp, ed., *Songgang kasa* (1959).
Kim Sŏng-bae *et al.*, eds., *Chuhae kasa munhak chŏnjip* ("Annotated Anthology of *Kasa* Poems") (1961).
Pak Sŏng-ŭi, *Nogye kasa t'onghae* ("The *Kasa* Poems of Nogye with Annotations") (1957).
Song Si-yong, ed., *Hanyang ka* (1949).
Yi Sang-bo, ed., *Kaego Pak Nogye yŏn'gu* ("A Revised Study of the Poetry of Pak Nogye") (1962).

Ch'oe Chin-wŏn, "Songgang kwa Kosan ŭi sigyŏng" ("The Poetic World of Songgang and Kosan"), *SGTN*, III (1958), 122-135.
Chŏng Chu-dong, "Kwansujae Hong Kye-yŏng kwa kŭŭi kasa *Hŭisŏl*" ("The *Hŭisŏl*, a *Kasa* Poem by Hong Kye-yŏng"), *KK*, 17 (1957), 29-42.
Hong Chae-hyo, "Udam Ch'ae Tŭk-ki wa *Ch'ŏndae pyŏlgok* e taehayŏ" ("On the *Ch'ŏndae pyŏlgok* by Ch'ae Tŭk-ki"), *KK*, 22 (1960), 50-56.
Kim Pong-yŏng, ed., "*Ch'imgoeng kasa* samp'yŏn" ("On the Three Poems in the *Ch'imgoeng kasa*"), *KK*, 20 (1959), 33-37.
Kim Sa-yŏp, "*Songgang kasa* sin'go" ("A New Study of the *Songgang kasa*"), *KTN*, II (1958), 3-42.

————————, "Tohakcha ŭi kagokkwan" ("The View of Poetry Held by Confucian Writers"), *KTN*, I (1956), 1-41.

Kim Tong-uk, "Hŏ Kang ŭi *Sŏho pyŏlgok* kwa Yang Sa-ŏn ŭi *Miin pyŏlgok*" ("Hŏ Kang's *Sŏho pyŏlgok* and Yang Sa-ŏn's *Miin pyŏlgok*"), *KK*, 25 (1962), 47-65.

Mun Chu-sŏk, "*Hanyang ka* yŏn'gu" ("A Study of the 'Song of Seoul' "), *Suktae hakpo*, 1 (1955), 219-244.

Nam Kwang-u, *Kugŏhak nonmunjip* (1962), pp. 347-360.

Pang Chong-hyŏn, "Nogye *kasa*" ("The *Kasa* Poems of Nogye"), *HG*, 118 (1956), 38-43.

————————, "*Songdam kasa* yŏn'gu" ("A Study of the *Songdam kasa*"), *CM*, III/7 (1958), 225-229.

Sin Tong-yŏp, "Sigasang ŭiro pon Song Myŏnang kwa Chŏng Songgang" ("The Poetic Friendship between Song Sun and Chŏng Ch'ŏl") *HG*, 106 (1956), 36-50.

Sŏ Su-saeng, "Songgang ŭi chŏnhu *Sa miin kok* ŭi yŏn'gu" ("Chŏng Ch'ŏl's Two 'Hymns of Constancy' "), *KTN*, VI (1962), 203-262.

Yi Ka-wŏn, ed., "*Moktong mundap ka*" ("Song of the Shepherd"), *HM*, III/11 (1957), 246-251.

Yi Pyŏng-gi, "*Pyŏl samiin kok* kwa *Sok samiin kok* e taehayŏ" ("On the *Pyŏl samiin kok* and *Sok samiin kok*"), *KK*, 15 (1956), 116-123.

Yi Sang-bo, "*Kwansŏ pyŏlgok* yŏn'gu" ("A Study of the *Kwansŏ pyŏlgok*"), *KK*, 26 (1963), 54-76.

Yi T'ae-gŭk, "Sae *kasa* ŭi hanain *Hwaga* e taehayŏ" ("On the Newly Discovered *Kasa* Poem, *Hwaga*"), *KK*, 24 (1961), 52-58.

Yun Chae-ch'ŏn, "Sibi *kasa* yŏn'gu ch'o" ("On the So-called Twelve *Kasa*"), *Mungyŏng*, 7 (1959), 60-86.

Translations

Lee, Peter H., *Kranich am Meer*, pp. 91-103.

————————, "The *Kasa* Poems of Pak In-no: Their Place in the History of Korean Poetry," *Oriens Extremus*, X (1963), 217-259.

————————, "The *Songgang Kasa* of Chŏng Ch'ŏl," *T'oung Pao*, XLIX (1961), 149-193.

————————, *Anthology of Korean Poetry*, pp. 73-74, 93-106, 108-110, 111-120, 149-153.

VII. Fiction in Chinese

Although the novel in the modern sense began only in the second quarter of the seventeenth century in Korea, its ancestors — legends, anecdotal narratives, and tales — are as old as human history itself. In Korea, however, where Chinese literature had a strong hold among the literati and where the proper system of writing in Korean developed only in the fifteenth century, it is not surprising that earlier surviving examples of fiction were strongly influenced by Chinese fiction and used the Chinese language as their medium.

There is a rich collection of folk tales in Korea in the form of fairy tales, novellas, hero tales, sagas, *pourquoi* stories,[1] myths, fables, legends, and jests. The oldest surviving examples of such tales are preserved in the *Samguk sagi* and *Samguk yusa* (see chap. i). The *Samguk yusa,* a collection of popular stories and folk tales, records a number of examples, foundation myths of Tangun, Puyŏ, and Karak and other unusual Buddhistic and Shamanistic stories. The book narrates the miraculous birth of the founders of ancient states (i.e., Chu Mong, Pak Hyŏkkŏse, and Kings T'arhae and Suro), generally from an egg, and their marriages (Tangun, Aryŏng, T'arhae, and Tohwanyŏ); hero tales (T'arhae, Suro, Hogong); and other etiological tales. The *Samguk sagi,* though an official dynastic history, contains many such stories in the section on biographies (chaps. 41-50), especially in chapters 45, 47, and 48 — stories of fictitious figures or the adventures and superhuman deeds of historical personages. Collections of unusual stories of folk origin, such as the *Hwarang segi* ("Chronicle of the *Hwarang*"), by Kim Tae-mun (fl. 702-737) and *Sui chŏn* ("Strange Stories"), by Pak Il-lyang (d. 1096), are no longer extant in their entirety, but nine stories have survived, finding their way into several other books.

In the Koryŏ dynasty, story collectors were lower governmental officials (*p'aegwan*)[2] who were hired by the court to gather anecdotes and strange stories circulating among the people to be used as reference materials for administration. Collectors of such stories not only gleaned the stories from among the people, but also added a personal touch to the stories to make them more entertaining or didactic. In the Koryŏ dynasty, from the middle of the

[1] See Stith Thompson, *The Folktale* (New York, 1946), p. 9.

[2] In Korea, they were lower officials. For the origin of the *p'aegwan* (pai-kuan in Chinese) and their function see *Han shu,* XXX, 0435d.

thirteenth century, story collecting became a vogue. First, with the importation of the Six Dynasties tales, T'ang *ch'uan-ch'i* (tales of the marvelous), and
Sung and Yüan collections of stories, collectors were encouraged to gather the
new material from among their own people for new stories.[3]

Second was the intention of story collectors to write down the great body
of oral tradition handed down from the previous kingdom. Third, the literati
away from the court recorded or invented such stories as a pastime, and their
books are primary sources for our study. Collections of essays by famous
scholar-statesmen contain such current popular stories in Chinese, of which
the first example is the *Paegun sosŏl* ("Stories of White Cloud"), by Yi
Kyu-bo (1168-1241). The *P'ahan chip* (1214), by Yi In-no (1152-1220), friend
of Yi Kyu-bo, is primarily a collection of Chinese verse by scholars, but also
records poetic tales, diaries, Silla anecdotes, and the current scenes and manners of Kaesŏng and P'yŏngyang. The third is the *Pohan chip* (1254), by Ch'oe
Cha (1188-1260), which contains popular stories current in towns, interesting
historical incidents, stories of *kisaeng* and the like. The *Yŏgong p'aesŏl*
(1342), by Yi Che-hyŏn, also records strange and humorous stories and character sketches.

Another type of story, which shows a definite advance in the development
of fiction, is the "personified story," in which the writer speaks through the
lips of a person already deceased or endows inanimate objects (wine, coin,
paper) and living things (bamboo, tadpole, turtle) with human attributes or
feelings. Stories belonging to this class occupy a transitional period in which
anecdotes and legends paved the way for real fiction. These stories used the
technique of personification chiefly as a vehicle of social criticism. The
Kuksun chŏn ("Story of Wine") of Im Ch'un (d. 1170) has as its theme the
rise and fall of the household of Kuk Sun ("Mr. Yeast Good Wine"). The
story is strongly autobiographical and contains a satire on the current political
instability. It also admonishes persons given to wine, and the hero's downfall
owing to the odor of his breath from wine and his subsequent illness and death
are clearly didactic. His second book, the *Kongbang chŏn* ("Story of Coins"),
personifies coins and deals with their mintage and usage, while indirectly criti-
cizing the current economic conditions in the country. Yi Kyu-bo wrote two
books in this tradition. One, the *Kuk sŏnsaeng chŏn* ("Story of Mr. Yeast"),
is similar in form and content to the *Kuksun chŏn*. The other personifies a
turtle and praises a scholar's integrity and loftiness in his refusal to accept an
offer from the court. The story is didactic and recommends moral cultivation
above all. The *Chuk puin chŏn* ("Story of Bamboo") is by Yi Kok (1298-1351),

---

[3]The importation of Chinese books dates back to the beginning of our history. The *Shan-hai ching* ("Book of the
Mountains and Rivers") was introduced to Paekche sometime in the third century, and *San-kuo chih* ("History of
the Three Kingdoms") to Koguryŏ sometime later. The *Sou-shen chi* ("Reports on Spiritual Manifestations") was
imported to Koryŏ before 1091, and *ch'ing t'an* (pure discussions) literature at or about the same time. The *T'ai-p'ing
kuang-chi* ("Extensive Records made in the Period of Great Peace") was already a popular book among the Koreans
of the early twelfth century, and one extant Koryŏ poem sings of this book.

father of Yi Saek (1328-1396), who was one of the most famous scholars of Koryŏ. The book is again didactic and praises the virtue of woman and satirizes the disorderly sexual relations of the time. Yi Ch'ŏm's *Chŏsaeng chŏn* ("Story of Paper") personifies paper and recommends honest admonitions to officials and encourages good administration. The *Chŏng sija chŏn* ("Tadpole Story"), written by a monk, Sigyŏngam, personifies a tadpole and is a satire on Buddhism and its clergy. This book introduces dialogue and current personages.

Buddhism, which flourished from the sixth to the fourteenth century as the state religion, gave rise to religious tales and lives of famous priests and their miracles. Among the best known is the anonymous *Wangnang panhon chŏn* ("Reincarnation of Mr. Wang"), believed to have been compiled in its present form sometime during the reign of King Sukchong (1661-1675-1720). The book reveals in realistic language the power of the Buddha and urges living beings to become devout believers in the religion. In plot and technique this is a short story. Woodblocks used for printing it are preserved in the Tonghwa and Haein Temples.

In the Yi dynasty, collections of tales and anecdotes (*p'aegwan munhak*) continued to be produced. Ŏ Suk-kwŏn (fl. 1554) in his *P'aegwan chapki* ("Miscellaneous Notes of a Storyteller") lists books of this kind, including the *Yongjae ch'onghwa,* by Sŏng Hyŏn (1439-1504). This famous collection of literary essays, historical tales, and character sketches, excellent in style and narrative technique, is especially admired for brilliance of characterization and for criticism of past and contemporary artistic circles. Sŏ Kŏ-jŏng's *T'aep'yŏng hanhwa kolgye chŏn* ("Peaceful Leisure Stories of Humor") was written in 1477 and published in or about 1482. A collection of "risqué" stories, the *Kogŭm soch'ong* ("Humorous Stories, Ancient and Modern"), believed to have been compiled by Song In (1517-1584), contains three separate books written from the time of King Sŏngjong to that of King Injo (1595-1623-1649).

The *Lieh-nü chuan* ("Stories of Famous Women") was imported to Korea in 1404 and translated into Korean in 1543. But the Chinese fiction which exercised most influence in fifteenth-century Korea was the *Chien-teng hsin-yü,* by Ch'ü Yü (d. 1433), imported sometime between 1421 and 1465. Kim Si-sŭp (1435-1493), the first significant writer of imaginative narrative, wrote his immortal *Kŭmo sinhwa* ("New Stories of the Golden Turtle") influenced by the *Chien-teng hsin-yü.* Only the first book, containing five stories, survives. This book enjoyed a great popularity in Korea as well as in Japan, where it was reprinted in 1653 and 1884. The stories in this book differ from those of Koryŏ in two respects: first, the scenes are set in Korea, whereas the older stories chose invariably China and Chinese characters; second, the endings are tragic, in contrast to the happy endings of stories produced previously. The *Kŭmo sinhwa,* unparalleled in beauty of expression and richness of local color, is indeed a masterpiece in the tradition of the tales of the marvelous.

In the category of personified stories, Im Che (1549-1587) was an outstanding writer. His *Hwasa* ("Story of Flowers") satirizes party strife at court. In the kingdom of flowers, he takes the role of a historian to recount the Confucian view of the virtuous sovereign and his loyal subjects. Im's *Susŏng chi* ("Story of Grievance Castle") expresses the discontent and pent-up grievances of a man who has to live in a society which does not promote people according to their qualifications. The fall of Grievance Castle and the subsequent reappearance of a happy world at the end of the story reflect the author's wishes for improving the political situation of his day. Here Im Che wishes to cleanse society of its evils, to reject treacherous retainers and to give opportunity to loyal subjects for a better government. The last work of this kind worthy of mention is the *Ch'ŏn'gun yŏnŭi* ("Romance of the Heavenly Lord"), by Chŏng T'ae-je (1612-1669). The book, consisting of thirty-one chapters, is an allegory on the working of the mind, based on the idealism of Chu Hsi.

A third class of stories consists of satirical tales. The *Hŏsaeng chŏn* ("Story of Mr. Hŏ"), by Pak Chi-wŏn (1737-1805), is a satire on the impracticality and useless book-learning of scholars. Hŏsaeng, Mr. Hŏ, a lover of books, made his wife starve for seven years as a result of his preparation for the civil service examination. But one day, admonished by his wife, he changes his mind, becomes a good businessman, and soon monopolizes the fruit and horsehair trade. Thieves attack him to rob him of his wealth, but he advises them to join him and make money. He then buys ships and transports the poor to a remote desert island where he builds a classless Utopia. He also monopolizes overseas trade and finally returns to the capital in triumph. His friend, who once made him a loan for his business, introduces him to a general who is searching for an able statesman. Mr. Hŏ gives him a series of lectures concerning administration, but disappears without trace on the day when the general and his friend come to his home to confer rank upon him.

The author, Pak Chi-wŏn, was one of the great champions of practical learning in the eighteenth century, and we can trace in this story the plans for social and economic improvements he had outlined for Korea. First he severely satirizes the literati class which indulges in empty talk. The monopoly of fruit and horsehair is significant. Fruit was used by the upper class as offerings in ancestor worship and on ceremonial occasions, and horsehair for making the caps they wore. Mr. Hŏ of the story empties the pockets of the literati and redistributes the contents among the poor. Here the author is attacking empty etiquette and ceremonies and the imposing of heavy, unjust taxes on the lower classes. Mr. Hŏ's motto to the thieves, "Get rich first, study later," implies that one must first deal with economic distress realistically in order to relieve the poor and save the country from hardships. He also stresses the importance of overseas trade as a measure for enriching the country. Finally his horror of the exploitation of the poor by the rich in the rigid Yi society is expressed in his creation of a Utopia. The book also advocates studies abroad as a measure for importing Western learning, the abolition of white clothes, and the cutting of hair. Pak's other stories which have as their theme the hypocrisies of the upper class are the *Hojil* ("Tiger's Rebuke") and *Yangban chŏn* ("Story of the Literati"). Two short stories, the *Kwangmun chŏn* ("Kwangmun the Beggar") and *Yedŏk sŏnsaeng chŏn* ("Story of Mr. Yedŏk") deal with lower-class people. The hero of the former story is a young beggar boy living by the Ch'ŏnggye River in the capital who, after many hardships, finally wins recognition and becomes a faithful employee in an apothecary shop. The latter is in the form of a *conte*, dealing with the true friendship between a scholar, Sŏngyulcha, and an old man of lower birth, Mr. Ŏm, a night-soil man. The story praises the righteous and virtuous deeds of Mr. Ŏm and condemns the hypocritical life of the upper class. Our author has to his credit several other stories, but they are variations on the same theme, satires on upper-class life. Pak was himself from the upper class. In his stories he was not so much interested in advocating the overthrow of his class as in appealing to its members for self-examination and for criticism of their blind resistance to practical learning. What he satirizes is, therefore, not the *yangban* class itself, but the *yangban's* obstinate conservatism and exploitation of the lower classes. Though his stories are in Chinese, the plot and scenes are laid in Korea and materials are derived from the real life of the time.

Stories and novels bearing in their titles the Chinese logograph for "dream" ("mong" in Korean) were among the most popular love stories in the Yi dynasty. The first novel of this type, the *Kuun mong* ("Cloud Dream of the Nine"), written in pure Korean, will be discussed in the next chapter. The second such novel, the *Ongnu mong* ("Dream of the Jade Chamber"), was written probably by Nam Yŏng-no in Chinese in the time of King Sukchong. It is a long work of sixty-four chapters. The hero, Mun Ch'ang-sŏng, in the celestial world is condemned to the earth for playing with five angels in the Jade Chamber. Born as a mortal with the name Yang Ch'ang-gok, the hero meets a famous *kisaeng,* Kang Nam-hong, who is one of the five angels also condemned to earthly life. They fall in love and vow marriage, but fate decrees otherwise. Yang passes the civil service examination and obtains the coveted *chinsa*[4] degree. But he marries the virgin Yun, another of the five condemned angels, and then is exiled on a false charge to a remote place where he meets yet another angel. When the country is invaded by barbarians, Yang leads his troops to repulse the enemy, which is led by no other than the hero's

---

[4] Corresponding to the modern "doctor of literature," this degree is taken before proceeding to the final civil service examination *(munkwa).*

mistress. The invasion force is defeated, and during the course of the combat, one of the enemy general's daughters, also a fallen angel, falls in love with the hero. The hero takes her to the capital on his triumphant return to the court. After leading a prosperous life with his two legally married wives and three concubines, the hero is finally reinstated in heaven with the five fallen angels. In its plot and scenes, which are laid in southern China, the *Ongnu mong* owes much to the *Kuun mong*.

Another love story written in Chinese, the *Hongbaekhwa chŏn* ("Story of Pink and White Flowers"), is by an anonymous hand. In the Ming dynasty there lived two close friends, Kye Tong-yŏng and Sun Kyŏng-hwa. Kye had a son, Ilchi, Sun had a daughter, Chikso. The parents arranged for their marriage in their childhood. But upon the death of Mr. Kye, Mr. Sun changed his mind and promised his daughter to a son of Minister Yŏ. Chikso then set out to search for her former fiancé, disguised as a man. She wandered about for many thousands of miles and came to live in the household of a certain Mr. Sŏl, with whose daughter she vowed matrimony. Chikso went to the capital under the pretext of taking the civil service examination and met the most successful candidate, Ilchi, her fiancé. But the emperor had already decided to wed his daughter to Ilchi. Chikso visited the princess and revealed her whole story, whereupon the princess consented to marry the son of Minister Yŏ instead. Chikso and Ilchi were married and lived a hundred years.

VIII. Fiction in Korean

We have mentioned that the *Kŭmo sinhwa* marks the first stage of the novel in the literary history of Korea, besides being an outstanding example of the tales of the marvelous (*ch'uan-ch'i*) tradition. Although stories and novels continued to be written in Chinese, it was not until the seventeenth century that the novel attained a distinct form as a genre. At about the same time writers began to write novels in pure Korean, using the new alphabet, evidently to meet the taste of the growing public. Historically, the second and third stages of the novel during its period of growth coincide with political and social changes in the country. After the Japanese and Manchu invasions, the middle class began to awake. The upper-class literati had betrayed their inefficiency in handling national affairs, and the middle- and lower-class people began to re-evaluate the past and look to the future with fresh perspectives. A new literary movement liberated writers from the restrictions of Neo-Confucianism, which had stifled emotional development and spontaneous expressions of life. New novelists were driven to reveal their innermost experiences in native rhythm adequate to encompass the richness and complexities of indigenous culture. Changes in form and emphasis in the novel were, therefore, related to changes in attitude toward "man" and his manners and destiny. The rise of the novel coincides with the diffusion of education, the increased social and economic consciousness of the middle class, and the rise of practical learning. Nevertheless, the development of plot, characterization, setting, and tone was also made possible by a constant flow of Chinese novels, among which the most influential were the *Shui hu chuan* ("Water Margin") and *San-kuo-chih yen-i* ("Romance of the Three Kingdoms").

The second landmark in the Korean novel was achieved by Hŏ Kyun (1569-1618), author of the *Hong Kiltong chŏn*[1] ("Life of Hong Kiltong"), perhaps the first novel written in Korean, which is reminiscent of the picaresque[2] novel in Europe, especially the German *Räuberroman*. As an illegitimate son of Minister Hŏ Yŏp, the author was keenly aware of his inferior status and

[1]A basic text is the Kyŏngp'an edition printed in woodblocks, consisting of twenty-four sheets; a photolithographic edition was published by Ewha Womans University in 1961. There are also several woodblock editions, a manuscript copy, and a number of modern reprints. See Chŏng Chu-dong, *Hong Kiltong chŏn yŏn'gu* (Taegu, 1961), pp. 141-147, reviewed by Kim Tong-uk in *AY*, V/1 (1962), 205-209. For summaries, paraphrases, or extracts of the Kiltong story in English see: H. N. Allen, *Korean Tales* (New York and London, 1889), pp. 170-193; Berta Metzger, *Tales Told in Korea* (New York, 1932), pp. 49-74; Zŏng In-sŏb, *Folk Tales from Korea* (London, 1952), pp. 207-223.

[2]Cf. C. Guillén, "Toward a Definition of the Picaresque," *Proceedings of the IIIrd Congress of the International Comparative Literature Association* (The Hague, 1962), pp. 252-266.

from his childhood displayed an interest in social revolution. As an active organizer of reform movements, he was captured and executed on a charge of treason. The hero of the story, Hong Kiltong, an illegitimate son of Minister Hong, has aspirations similar to those of the author, and the setting is laid in contemporary society, the time of King Sejong. Hong suffers all manners of maltreatment from members of his family, including his father's concubine Ch'onan. In a fit of jealousy over the minister's love for Kiltong's mother and his growing interest in the child, Ch'onan bribes a fortune-teller and a shaman priestess to inform the minister that Kiltong will commit fratricide if allowed to grow up, and she also hires an assassin to kill him. Upon hearing the croaking of a crow during his study of the *Book of Changes* in his mountain retreat, Kiltong divines the imminent danger, transforms himself into a boy riding on donkey, and punishes the assassin and the fortune-teller. After reporting to his father the evil scheme against his life and its outcome, he sets out on a roving journey. Deep in the mountains he encounters a band of thieves, passes their test of strength by lifting and hurling a huge rock, and thereby becomes their leader. He then leads the thieves in an attack on Haein Temple, which has become an asylum for wicked officials and corrupt monks. By an ingenious trick played upon the monks, Kiltong and his men seize the treasures hidden in the Temple. After this exploit, Hong calls his band the Hwalbindang, whose aim is the deliverance of the poor, and mocks every sanctity of bureaucracy and of the authoritarian world.

He then tours the eight provinces of the country, seizes wealth unjustly exacted by rapacious officials, and distributes it among the poor. His expedition reaches a climax when he humiliates the greedy governor of Hamgyŏng province and escapes with grain and weapons. With the government forces in hot pursuit, he makes seven straw figures, infuses spirit into them, and dispatches them to the eight provinces. After each province has brought its captured "Kiltong" to the court, it is found that all eight men look alike in every respect. Kiltong explains to the king the evil practice of discrimination against illegitimate children and promises to leave Korea in ten years, if the king does not arrest him. At that moment, the eight men fall flat on the ground, turning out to be eight straw puppets. Shortly thereafter, Kiltong posts a notice on the four gates of the capital to the effect that if the government made him Minister of War he would surrender. Upon appointment to the post, Kiltong appears in person, thanks the king, soars high up among the clouds, and goes striding upon the wind. The king, deeply moved by his talent, pardons him.

Kiltong then sails off for an island near Nanking. After an adventure on Mangdang Mountain on Che Island, he conquers Yul Island in the South and builds a classless Utopia. After reigning thirty years he dies at the age of seventy-two,[3] leaving behind three sons and two daughters.

[3]Seventy-two is a mystic number in Chinese thought. For example, Confucius is said to have had seventy-two disciples, and Liu Pang, the founder of the Han dynasty, seventy-two black moles on his left thigh.

This work is clearly a "problem" novel. Though inspired by the *Shui hu chuan,* it is inferior to its Chinese model in plot and characterization. There still are elements of the *ch'uan-ch'i* in such episodes as the miraculous removal of grain from government granaries. It is also strongly autobiographical, and the hero is the ideal of the author. The *Hong Kiltong chŏn* advances the following ideas; abolition of the class system, especially as it includes discrimination against illegitimate sons; eradication of the contradictions inherent in contemporary society; liquidation of wealth unjustly amassed by avaricious officials and underlings; overseas emigration of the Korean people; anti-Buddhism, as implied in the hero's attack on and plundering of the Haein Temple. Another sociological novel is the anonymous *Chŏn Uch'i chŏn* ("Life of Chŏn Uch'i").[4]

The historical novel, chiefly dealing with the personages and events during the Japanese and Manchu invasions, is a distinct type of fiction in the Yi period. Most of the historical novels are anonymous, and can be divided into the historical romance and the historical novel proper. Historical romances are mostly influenced by the *San-kuo-chih yen-i* and are invariably set in China. Even their narrative technique, especially the beginning and end of each chapter, is strongly reminiscent of the Chinese model. Hyperbolical descriptions appearing in the Chinese model reappear in their character sketches. Description of the hero is often limited to that of physical appearance, seldom given to the psychological aspect. Heroes are often masters in astronomy, military tactics, and magic, and their rise is mostly foretold by children's songs.[5] Buddhism, Taoism, and Confucianism underlie the thought of these romances — especially Taoism.

In the *Imjin nok* ("Record of the Year 1592"), by an anonymous hand, famous generals who fought against the Japanese become heroes of the book. Events related to them are often not historical. The *Yu Ch'ungnyŏl chŏn* ("Exploits of Yu Ch'ungnyŏl"), *Cho Ung chŏn* ("Story of Cho Ung"), *Chang Kukchin chŏn* ("Story of Chang Kukchin"), and *Kwŏn Ikchung chŏn* ("Story of Kwŏn Ikchung") are some of the representative works of this type. Structurally, the last two consist of two parts, the first part dealing with the love or marriage of the hero, and the second with his military exploits.

The *Im Kyŏngŏp chŏn* ("Story of Im Kyŏngŏp") and *Pakssi chŏn* ("Life of Lady Pak"), on the other hand, are examples of historical fiction proper. The former is a story of General Im, who repulsed the Manchu invaders but was murdered by a villainous retainer, Kim Cha-jŏm. The latter deals with Yi Sibaek (1592-1660) and his wife, née Pak, who distinguished themselves during the Manchu invasion. This book lays stress on the wife's accomplishment in magic. A woman who saves the state in a great crisis later becomes a type

[4]Zŏng, pp. 224-234.

[5]Cf. Robert Ruhlmann, "Traditional Heroes in Chinese Popular Fiction," *The Confucian Persuasion,* ed. Arthur F. Wright (Stanford, 1960), pp. 141-176.

in such historical fiction. This was a technique to attract women, who were the novel-reading public of the day.[6]

The court novels belong to historical fiction proper. The *Kyech'uk ilgi* ("Kyech'uk Diary") is a court diary written by an anonymous court lady. The book, consisting of two parts, records in realistic language the political upheavals and court intrigues between the years 1609 and 1623, especially the tyrant Kwanghae's misgovernment and his massacre of the family of Queen Mother Inmok. The heroine of the novel is the queen mother herself (1584-1632), and the persecutions she suffered and her secluded life are the main themes. The *Hanjung nok* ("A Record of Sorrowful Days," 1795-1805) is actually a book of court diaries, but is sufficiently artistic to be read as a novel. The author is Princess Hyegyŏng (1735-1815), née Hong, the consort of Prince Sado (1735-1762), son of King Yŏngjo. The king was estranged from his son, who, owing to the king's persecution, became insane and died a cruel death at the age of twenty-eight. Princess Hyegyŏng, who had to spend the rest of her life in seclusion and sorrow, wrote down her memories in epistolary form, the first part in 1795, in her sixty-first year, and second and third parts in 1805 for the reading of King Sunjo (1790-1801-1834). The book records in simple but moving language the cause of the death of Prince Sado, her secluded life after his death, and the persecutions she suffered at the hands of treacherous slanderers. Contemporary court life is vividly described in court language which abounds in graceful turns of speech and honorifics. The *Inhyŏn wanghu chŏn* ("Tale of Queen Inhyŏn") is an anonymous story of court intrigue involving two queens. After the death of the first queen, King Sukchong marries Queen Inhyŏn (1667-1701). Being unable to bear an heir, the queen asks the king to take a certain lady, Chang, as a concubine. After bearing a son, Lady Chang intrigues to advance herself to the position of queen, and finally succeeds and expels Queen Inhyŏn. The king feels remorse, and when Lady Chang's faction murders most of the deposed queen's supporters, he reinstates Inhyŏn as queen and kills Lady Chang.

The period of the maturity of the novel is marked by Kim Man-jung (1637-1692) and his two extant novels. His *Kuun mong* ("Cloud Dream of the Nine," 1687-1688),[7] the third landmark in the Korean novel, was written at the place

---

[6]The role played by women readers in the rise of vernacular fiction has been little studied. For a parallel phenomenon taking place in eighteenth-century England Addison remarks in the *Guardian*, No. 155 (Tuesday, September 8, 1713), a periodical started by Steele in March 1713 and discontinued in October of the same year: "There are some reasons why learning seems more adapted to the female world than to the male. As, in the first place, because they have more spare time upon their hands, and lead a more sedentary life . . . . A second reason why women should apply themselves to useful knowledge rather than men, is, because they have the natural gift of speech in greater perfection . . . . There is another reason why those especially who are women of quality should apply themselves to letters; namely, because their husbands are generally strangers to them."

[7]There are three woodblock editions, one in Chinese (1803) and two in Korean (1862, 1920); seven manuscript copies of which three are dated (1846, 1885, 1907); two editions printed in movable type, one in Chinese with Korean connectives (1911) and another in pure Korean (1913). The manuscript copy owned by Yi Ka-wŏn is considered to be the best in Korean, other copies being derivations from it. James S. Gale, in preparing his English translation, used the 1803 edition and a Korean edition, conjectured to have been the source for the Yi Ka-wŏn copy. There are also a Japanese interlinear edition (1916) and a Japanese translation, as well as numerous modern editions printed after 1913. In view of the lack of any convincing evidence that the work was written originally in Korean, the 1803 edition in Chinese is generally considered to be a basic text, perhaps derived from an authentic text no longer extant.

of his exile, Sŏnch'ŏn, to console his ailing mother. Kim was an archpriest of the movement to keep the Korean language undefiled and to use Korean instead of Chinese in literary works. The plot of the *Kuun mong* is laid in T'ang China, and the novel is a romantic tale of the Buddhist idea of resignation, that all fame and glories of the human world are but a dream. A Buddhist saint, Taeyŏ (Great Master Yukkwan), sends out his best disciple, Sŏngjin, on an errand to the Dragon King of Tungt'ing Lake. At the same time a fairy matron sends her eight fairies to the master to inquire after his health. On the way home, Sŏngjin meets the eight fairies, with whom he frolics till sunset. As a punishment he is sent to the Ruler of the Underworld, who takes pity on him and causes him to be born in a certain Yang family in Suju, with the name Yang So-yu. The eight fairies, too, are condemned to earth as human beings. They are born beautiful girls and grow up to be either famous *kisaeng* or daughters of respectable families. The hero establishes himself as a man of fame, securing a high position at court after passing the civil service examination. Various romances develop one after another as the hero meets all of the eight women. Thus, the hero who was reborn in the human world enjoys the pleasures of man with eight fairies who were condemned to the human world. One September afternoon, he climbs the hill west of his palace with his wives, each of whom wears a spray of chrysanthemum in her hair. They enjoy the autumn scenery, passing a cup back and forth among them. When the sun casts a shadow on the mountains and the clouds spread darkness over the plains, he takes out a jade flute and begins to play. Overcome with sorrow by the plaintive tune, the two wives turn to him and ask him why he looks so dejected. So-yu answers:

> To the north I see a lonely peak standing amid a stretch of wide plains and the A-fang Palace of the First Emperor which stands amid the glow of twilight and entangled weeds; to the west a dreary wind stirs the forest as the evening clouds descend on the Mou Tomb of the Warrior Emperor of Han; to the east I see the painted walls mirrored in the sky and red roofs soaring skyward. The moon comes and goes over the deserted, jade railings of the Palace of Splendor and Purity where once Emperor Hsüan-tsung frolicked with his Precious Consort Yang. All were once sovereigns of great renown; but where are they now? I, So-yu, a small scholar from the land of Ch'u, have received great favors from the throne and I have risen to the rank of a general and of a minister. Morever, the members of my family have lived together in harmony, and our deep affection increases as we advance in age. How could this have been were it not for the affinity of a former existence? Once we die, however, lofty towers will crumble, crystal lakes will go dry, and our palace where we sing and dance today will be covered with weeds and lapped by the cold mist. Woodcutters and cowherds will, then, tell our mournful story, saying, 'This is where Master Yang frolicked with his eight wives. His wealth and elegance, the jade faces and flowery bearings of his wives are gone, gone forever.' Those woodcutters and cowherds will look upon this place just as I look upon the palaces and tombs of the ancient emperors. When I think of it, a man's life is nothing but the span of a moment.

He then comprehends the essence of the three religions (Confucianism, Buddhism, and Taoism) and chooses Buddhism as the path to his salvation. He returns with the eight fairies to his master, becomes a bodhisattva, and enters the Promised Land. The tenets of the three religions are incorporated into the texture of this novel, which can be said to afford an interesting indication of the current social attitude toward three ways of thought. Confucian bureaucracy was mainly identified with realistic and utilitarian pursuits, Taoism with Epicureanism, and Buddhism with quietism and the renunciation of the world. Buddhism is, however, predominant, especially the workings of karma. The three worlds in Buddhism—past, present, and future—are well linked together to achieve coherence and artistic integrity. One critic offers another view: the book is a reflection of man's ideal *Weltanschauung* in authoritarian society.

Another novel by Kim, the *Sassi namjŏng ki* ("Story of Lady Sa," c. 1689-1692), is a satirical remonstrance against the institution of concubinage, allegedly against King Sukchong who gave ear to his concubine and banished Queen Inhyŏn, as recorded in the *Inhyŏn wanghu chŏn*. The setting is laid in Ming China, but the story is an exact parallel to that of Queen Inhyŏn. When one considers that the author was banished from the court for his opposition to the king's move to degrade the queen, the motive of the novel becomes transparent. This novel is inferior in plot and narration to the *Kuun mong,* but as a first domestic novel it set up a pattern for such later novels as the *Changhwa hongnyŏn chŏn* ("Tale of Rose Flower and Pink Lotus").[8]

Written by an anonymous hand, the *Changhwa hongnyŏn chŏn* is a story of a cruel stepmother who maltreats the two daughters of the flower names. The stepmother, in an attempt to slander her stepdaughters, hides a large skinned rat in their bed at night. Next morning the stepmother accuses one of having a miscarriage, and has the girl, Rose Flower, drowned in the river. The other girl, Pink Lotus, is informed of her sister's death in a dream, and following a blue bird, goes to the scene of the murder, where, in great grief, she plunges into the waters. The spirits of the two virgins then become malicious ghosts and frighten the magistrate of the province. The ghosts harass the people so much that a renowned warrior, Chŏng Tong-u (real name: Chŏng Tong-ho), is dispatched from the capital. When he meets them, the ghosts appeal to the warrior to punish their stepmother and cleanse their names. The stepmother is executed for her crime, and the bodies of the two daughters are reclaimed from the river and given a decent burial. Satisfied, the malicious ghosts are reborn again as two daughters to the father, who has married a virtuous woman. The parents and daughters live happily ever after.

The action of the *kongan* novel, as it is called, always takes place in a law court. The term means "public cases," covering stories of crime and detection, wherein an upright and wise magistrate, a guardian of the law and champion

[8]Zŏng, pp. 201-207.

of the people, solves a crime or settles a dispute.[9] The *Changhwa hongnyŏn chŏn* can be considered to be an example of this type, when the court investigates the petition of the ghosts of the two girls and decides to avenge the stepmother on their behalf. The *Chin Taebang chŏn* ("Story of Chin Taebang"), *Pak Munsu chŏn* ("Pak Munsu, The Royal Inspector"), and *Ongnangja chŏn* ("Ongnang the Virtuous Wife") belong to this group. These novels are chiefly didactic in tone, and the reproval of vice and promotion of virtue is a recurrent theme. The magistrate's sermon generally emphasizes the five principles of human conduct. Yet these novels are rich in description of the family life of the common people.

The masterpiece of the Korean novel is unequivocally the *Ch'unhyang chŏn* ("Life of Spring Fragrance"), by an anonymous hand, the most popular novel in Korea. Written sometime in the eighteenth century, the novel was expanded with new parts added during the course of reprintings so that the original version is difficult to trace. The novel is the story of a romance between the son of an upper-class family and the daughter of a socially despised *kisaeng*. A male servant of the hero is cast in the important role of spokesman for the common people of the time. During the reign of King Injo,[10] Yi Toryŏng (Yŏng), the son of a yangban, falls in love with Spring Fragrance, the *kisaeng* daughter, on a spring day in the Kwanghan Pavilion. After turning down the repeated overtures of the hero through his cunning and comical servant Pangja, Spring Fragrance finally yields. The hero, however, is soon ordered to accompany his father, who has been nominated Minister of Personnel,[11] to the capital. After a tearful scene of farewell in which they exchange tokens of remembrance, a mirror and a jade ring,[12] the couple pledge eternal love, the girl promising that she will wait forever for Yŏng's return. After the hero's departure for Seoul, the provincial governor,[13] enraptured by the beauty of Spring Fragrance, commands the mother of the girl to deliver her up as his concubine. The proposal firmly refused, the governor imprisons Spring Fragrance and subjects her to sadistic torture, which she endures with amazing fortitude. In the meantime, in the guise of a beggar, the hero returns to town to serve as the Secret Royal Inspector (*amhaeng ŏsa*) of the provincial administration.[14] Discovering the tragic fate of his beloved, he reveals his identity and hands out stern punishment to the governor and rescues the girl. They live happily ever after.[15]

---

[9]Compare, for example, plays and stories centering around Pao Cheng (999-1062), a Sung official, including a Yüan play *Hui-lan chi* ("Circle of Chalk") and a Ming story *Pao-kung an* ("The Case of Lord Pao") or *Lung-t'u kung-an* ("Cases of the Scholar of the Lung-t'u Pavilion"). In some cases, however, crimes solved by the magistrate are not always closely related to the central plot of the *kongan* stories.

[10]In the Wanp'an edition the events of the plot take place during the time of King Sukchong.

[11]In the Wanp'an edition he is nominated Sixth Royal Secretary.

[12]This episode is omitted in the Wanp'an edition.

[13]The Wanp'an edition identifies him as Pyŏn Hak-to.

[14]In the Kyŏngp'an edition Yŏng petitions for this role, while in the Wanp'an edition he is appointed by the king.

[15]According to the Wanp'an edition, Mongnyong rose to be Chief State Counselor and had three sons and two daughters, all of whom emulated the accomplishments of their father.

There are four editions printed in block letters, of which the Kyŏngp'an (printed in Seoul under the title of *Ch'unhyang chŏn*) and Wanp'an (printed in Chŏnju under the title of *Yŏllyŏ Ch'unhyang sujŏl ka*) editions are our reliable sources for this novel. Besides, there are more than ten manuscript copies and some thirty printed editions. The Wanp'an edition shows a later stage in the development of the novel than the Kyŏngp'an edition, differing from the latter in the following details: Spring Fragrance is not a *kisaeng* daughter but a girl from a middle-class family; Yi Toryŏng's name is changed from Yŏng to Mongnyong, the name used in all subsequent editions; Yi is engaged to Spring Fragrance only with the consent of her mother; Hyangdan, a servant girl, always accompanies Spring Fragrance; on the way to Namwŏn, Mongnyong meets a messenger dispatched by Spring Fragrance with a letter and learns of his beloved's imprisonment; and in the prison Spring Fragrance has an encouraging dream in which some of the virtuous and heroic women of China appear and console her. Furthermore, the Kyŏngp'an edition is in prose, and the Wanp'an edition is in verse, in the *kasa* form, chiefly meant to be sung or recited.

People of all classes hold that the *Ch'unhyang chŏn* is the ripest production of the Korean novel. It is. The Ch'unhyang story enjoyed a long evolution in the course of its development, and its "matter" is the property of all the people. Its source might have been a simple story current among the people about love and feminine virtue. But when an anonymous writer wrote it down in the eighteenth century, it became a book which epitomized the Korean people's manners and customs, dreams and beliefs of the time. The novel contains brilliant characters, who live in every reader's memory, and abounds in human and humorous action. Beautiful and virtuous Spring Fragrance and her devoted and shrewd *kisaeng* mother (Wŏlmae), passionate and upright Yi Toryŏng and his cunning yet loyal servant are masterly inventions. Yet Spring Fragrance's chastity and virtue suffuse the entire novel, giving a special reality and poignancy to the work. The people delight to see in Spring Fragrance a paragon of chastity and a model of the virtuous wife; but others also read the book for its protest against the privileged class and defense of human rights.

Except for a few imitations of the *Ch'unhyang chŏn* and some minor works, the classical novel entered its period of decline in the nineteenth century. One of the notable works of this period, however, is probably the anonymous *Imhwa Chŏngyŏn*. It presents altogether several hundred characters, of whom seventy are cast in important roles. The leading roles belong to four women, Im, Hwa, Chŏng, and Yŏn, all of whom are at the center of a human panorama of immense scope around the hero, Imsaeng. Other noteworthy titles are the *Ch'aebong kambyŏl kok* ("The Lament of Ch'aebong") and *Pae paejang chŏn* ("Story of Subcommander Pae"). The former is a mixture of novel and ballads; the latter employs much dramatic dialogue. The germ of the former was a dramatic narrative sung by a ballad singer. When written down in its present form as a novel, it became a satirical and humorous piece of literature.

We have omitted discussion of fables, children's stories (e.g., *K'ongjwi p'atchwi*)[16], and legends turned into novels (e.g., *Simch'ŏng chŏn*[17] and *Hŭngbu chŏn*[18]).

With the importation of Western civilization and culture toward the end of the Yi dynasty, traditional verse and prose forms rapidly gave way to new. Yi In-jik, the first writer of the new novel modeled after the Western style, will be discussed later.

[16]Metzger, pp. 181-196; William Elliot Griffis, *The Unmannerly Tiger and Other Korean Tales* (New York, 1911), pp. 87-95; Frances Carpenter, *Tales of a Korean Grandmother* (New York, 1947), pp. 121-124.

[17]Allen, pp. 152-169; Carpenter, pp. 81-86; Nikolay v. Kotschubey, *Koreanische Märchen* (Zürich, 1948), pp. 87-93; Metzger, pp. 120-133.

[18]Allen, pp. 89-115; Carpenter, pp. 222-228; Griffis, pp. 135-143; Kim So-un, *The Story Bag* (Rutland and Tokyo, 1957), pp. 145-153.

Bibliography: *Fiction in Chinese and in Korean*

Chang Tŏk-sun, *Kungmunhak t'ongnon* (1960), pp. 191-207, 235-324, 385-417, 430-447
Cho Yun-je, *Hanguk munhak sa* (1963), pp. 15-19, 43-48, 63-68, 103-106, 148-154, 241-264, 305-352.
──────────, *Kungmunhak kaesŏl* (1960), pp. 152-207.
Chu Wang-san, *Chosŏn kodae sosŏl sa* ("History of the Korean Novel") (1950).
Kim Ki-dong, *Hanguk kodae sosŏl kaeron* ("Outline of Classical Korean Novels") (1956).
──────────, *Yijo sidae sosŏl non* ("Essays in Yi Dynasty Novels") (1959).
Kim T'ae-jun, *Chosŏn sosŏl sa* ("History of the Korean Novel") (1933).
Ku Cha-gyun, *Hanguk p'yŏngmin munhak sa* ("History of Korean Plebeian Literature") (1955).
Pak Sŏng-ŭi, *Hanguk kodae sosŏl sa* ("History of Classical Korean Novels") (1958).

Studies in the Novel

Chang Ki-gŭn, "Chŏn'gi sosŏl kwa kŭ sŏngjang: sŏrhwa munhak ŭi chŏn'gae wa sosŏl rosŏŭi wansŏng" ("The Growth of the Tales of the Marvelous: the Development of Narrative Literature and the Perfection of the Novel"),*STN,* IX (1959), 221-269.
Chŏng Pyŏng-uk, *Kungmunhak san'go* (1960), pp. 212-221.
Kim Ham-dŭk, "Uri kungjŏng sosŏl ŭi sŏngkyŏk myosa sogo" ("The Character Sketch in the Court Novel"), *Suktae munhak,* 2 (1958), 204-218.
Kim Yŏng-suk, "Sado seja ŭi pigŭk kwa kŭŭi chŏngsin punsŏkhakchŏk koch'al" ("The Tragedy of Prince Sado and a Psychoanalytical Study of His Case"), *KK,* 19 (1958), 3-52.
Sin Ki-hyŏng, "Kajŏnch'e munhak non'go" ("A Study of Personified Tales in the Koryŏ Period"), *KK,* 15 (1956), 93-109; 17 (1957), 65-76.
──────────, "Hanguk sosŏl paltal tan'gye e issŏsŏŭi Chungguk sosŏl ŭi yŏnghyang" ("The Influence of Chinese Novels on the Development of the Korean Novel"), *KTN,* I (1956), 43-89.

Studies on Individual Works

Ewha Womans University Korean Literature Research Institute, *Hanguk kodae sosŏl ch'ongsŏ* ("A Collection of Classical Korean Novels"), 1 (1958), 2 (1959), 3 (1960), 4 (1961).
Kang Han-yŏng, ed., *Kyech'uk ilgi* (1958).
Kim Sam-bul, ed., *Pae paejang chŏn, Onggojip chŏn* (1950).
Mun Sŏn-gyu, ed., *Hwasa* (1961).
Pak Chi-wŏn, *Togang nok,* tr. Yi Yun-jae (1946).
Pak Sŏng-ŭi *"Kwangmunja chŏn* yŏn'gu" (A Study of the *Kwangmunja chŏn"), Inmun kwahak,* 7 (1962), 25-52.
_____, *"Kye sangguk chŏn* sogo" ("A Study of the *Kye sangguk chŏn"), Mulli nonjip,* VI (1962), 39-72.
Son Nak-pŏm, tr., *Hŭngbu chŏn* (1957).
_____, tr., *Pakssi puin chŏn* (1956).
Yi Ka-wŏn, *"Yangban chŏn* yŏn'gu" (A Study of the *Yangban chŏn"), TMY,* I (1963), 139-188.
Yi Min-su, *Yŏnam sŏnjip* ("Selections from Yŏnam's Tales") (1956).
Yi Myŏng-sŏn, tr., *Imjin nok* (1948).
Yi Pyŏng-gi and Kim Tong-uk, eds., *Hanjung nok* (1961).
Yi Pyŏng-gi, ed., *Ŭiyudang ilgi* (1948).
_____, *Yorowŏn yahwa ki* ("The Yorowŏn Tales") (1958).

Legends, Narratives, and Tales

Ch'oe Sang-su, *Chosŏn chimyŏng chŏnsŏl chip* ("Tales Connected with Place Names") (1947).
_____, *Chosŏn kubi chŏnsŏl chi* ("A Collection of Korean Oral Literature") (1949).
_____, *Chosŏn min'gan chŏnsŏl chip* ("A Collection of Korean Folk Tales") (1947).
_____, *Kyŏngju ŭi kojŏk kwa chŏnsŏl* ("Historic Remains and Legends of Kyŏngju") (1946).
_____, *Puyŏ ŭi kojŏk kwa chŏnsŏl* ("Historic Remains and Legends of Puyŏ) (1955).
Hong Sa-yong, *Paekche ŭi chŏnsŏl* ("Legends of Paekche") (1959).
Pak Kyŏng-wŏn, *Kyŏngnam ŭi kojŏk kwa munhwa* ("Historic Remains and Culture of South Kyŏngsang Province") (1955).
Son Chin-t'ae, *Chosŏn minjok munhwa ŭi yŏn'gu* ("Studies in Korean National Culture") (1948).
_____, *Chosŏn minjok sŏrhwa ŭi yŏn'gu* ("Studies in the Folklore of Korea") (1947).

Kim Si-sŭp

Chŏng Pyŏng-uk, *Kungmunhak san'go* (1960), pp. 222-237.
_____, "Kim Si-sŭp yŏn'gu" ("The Life and Thought of Kim Si-sŭp"), *STN,* VII (1958), 153-196.
Yi Ka-wŏn, tr., *Kŭmo sinhwa* (1953).

Hŏ Kyun

Chŏng Chu-dong, *Hong Kiltong chŏn yŏn'gu* ("Studies in the 'Life of Hong Kiltong' ") (Taegu, 1961).

Kim Man-jung

Chŏng Kyu-bok, *"Kuun mong ibon ko"* ("Different Editions of the *Kuun mong*"), *AY*, IV/2 (1961), 1-43; V/1 (1962), 133-159.

Pak Sŏng-ŭi, tr., *Kuun mong, Sassi namjŏng ki* (1959).

Yi Ka-wŏn, tr., *Kuun mong* (1955).

Ch'unhyang chŏn

Cho Yun-je, ed., *Ch'unhyang chŏn pu Ch'unhyang chŏn ibon ko* ("*Ch'unhyang chŏn*, with an Appendix on its Different Editions") (1962).

Kang Han-yŏng, ed., *P'ansori sasŏl Ch'unhyang ka*, Vol. 1 of the *Sin Chae-hyo chŏnjip* ("Collected Works of Sin Chae-hyo") (1962).

Yi Ka-wŏn, ed., *Ch'unhyang chŏn* (1957).

Kim Tong-uk, *"Ch'unhyang chŏn ibon ko"* ("On the Different Editions of the *Ch'unhyang chŏn*"), in *Thirtieth Anniversary Volume of Chungang University* (1955), pp. 265-315.

————————, *"Ch'unhyang chŏn paegyŏng ŭrosŏŭi Namwŏn ŭi chijijŏk koch'al"* ("A Geographical Study of Namwŏn as a Background to the *Ch'unhyang chŏn*"), *YHS*, pp. 79-94.

————————, *"Ch'unhyang chŏn ŭi pigyojŏk yŏn'gu"* ("A Comparative Study of the *Ch'unhyang chŏn*"), *AY*, III/1 (1960), 81-128.

Ku Cha-gyun, "Kodaebon *Ch'unhyang chŏn*" ("Annotated Old Edition of the *Ch'unhyang chŏn*"), *Mulli nonjip*, III (1958), 419-444.

————————, "Kyŏngp'an *Ch'unhyang chŏn*" ("The Kyŏngp'an Edition of the *Ch'unhyang chŏn*"), *Mulli nonjip*, III (1958), 391-418.

Yi In-mo, *"Ch'unhyang chŏn ŭi munjang sŏngkyŏkhakchŏk sigo"* ("Masculine and Feminine Styles of Speech in the *Ch'unhyang chŏn*"), *Mulli nonjip*, V (1962), 49-88.

Translations

Allen, H. N., *Korean Tales* (New York and London, 1889).

Anonymous, *Fragrance of Spring*, tr. Chai Hong Sim (1962).

————————, *Le Bois Sec Refleuri*, tr. Hong Tyong-u (Paris, 1895).

————————, *The Tale of Shim Chung* (Pyongyang, 1958).

Carpenter, Frances, *Tales of a Korean Grandmother* (New York, 1947).

Ch'oe Sang-su, *Legends of Korea* (1951).

Chu Yo-sup, *The Forest of the White Cock: Tales and Legends of the Silla Period* (1962).

Eckardt, Andreas, *Unter dem Odongbaum: Koreanische Sagen, Märchen und Fabeln* (Eisenach, n.d.).

————————, *Die Ginsengwurzel: Koreanische Sagen, Volkserzählungen und Märchen* (Eisenach, 1955).

Griffis, William Elliot, *The Unmannerly Tiger and Other Korean Tales* (New York, 1911)

Im Pang and Yi Yuk, *Korean Folk Tales*, tr. James S. Gale (Rutland and Tokyo, 1963).

Kim Man-jung, *The Cloud Dream of the Nine*, tr. James S. Gale (London, 1922).

Kim So-un, *The Story Bag* (Rutland and Tokyo, 1957).

Kotschubey, Nikolay v., *Koreanische Märchen* (Zürich, 1948).

Metzger, Berta, *Tales Told in Korea* (New York, 1932).

Pak Tae-yong, *A Korean Decameron*, I (1961).

Zŏng In-sŏb, *Folk Tales from Korea* (London, 1952); reviewed by Peter H. Lee in *Comparative Literature*, VII (1955), 162-164.

IX. The Drama

Korean drama has its origin in the agricultural festivals of the primitive era. During such festivals as the Majigut, Saebŭlk, and Hanbŭlkch'um among the northern tribes and on similar occasions in the fifth and tenth moons among the southern tribes, the people drank, sang, and danced. The dances were performed to the rhythmic accompaniment of chorus or drums and other musical instruments. There is speculation that the people on such occasions may have worn masks — masks to threaten wild animals or masks of famous generals who distinguished themselves in tribal wars. We may see remnants of such mask dances in the lion dance of Pukch'ŏng, mask dance of Pongsan, and "five-actor play" *(Ogwan[g]dae)* of T'ongnyŏng, Pusan, Tongnae, Kosŏng, and Chinju.[1] On the fifteenth day of the first moon the people in Pukch'ŏng, wearing masks of different animals, march in a procession, headed by the lion. Accompanied by music they go through the village and gather money and rice which become communal property to be used later on occasions of marriage, funeral, famine, and flood. This dance is, however, conjectured to be of foreign origin.

Lack of records prevents a detailed study of ritual dances in Koguryŏ and Paekche. It is, however, established that among the three kingdoms Koguryŏ was the first to import Central Asian instruments. Koguryŏ music and dances were famous in Sui and T'ang as well as in Japan. The earliest record of the performance of "a hundred shows" by mimes, acrobats, jugglers, singers, and dancers in Silla occurs in the year A.D. 32. Another recorded instance of such festivals with dances and theatrical performances occurred in the year 551, in conjunction with the establishment of the harvest festival *(p'algwanhoe)* by King Chinhŭng.

A ritual symbolizing the conflict between the forces of life and death in Silla was a sword dance instituted in honor of their national hero, Knight Kwan Ch'ang, a *hwarang*. At the age of sixteen, Kwan Ch'ang, son of P'umil, participated in the invasion of Paekche as vice-commander of the Silla army, but was killed (660) by the equally famous Paekche general Kye Paek. In order

---

[1] Originated in a small village of Ch'ogye in Hapch'ŏn, South Kyŏngsang province. Tradition has it that during a flood villagers found a wooden box containing masks and a book. Subsequently disasters occurred year after year until they performed a play with the masks from the box according to the instructions in the book. About twenty masks are used in the play, which satirizes corrupt literati and apostate priests.

to praise his heroism and loyalty, the people initiated this dance lamenting the premature death of the knight. This dance seems to have been popular in the Koryŏ and Yi dynasties. The *Chŭngbo munhŏn pigo* ("Korean Encyclopaedia") adds that the sword dance was performed together with the Ch'ŏyong dance in later times.

The Ch'ŏyong was another famous dance in Silla. Ch'ŏyong, son of the Dragon King of the Eastern Sea, exorcised evil spirits by song and dance (879). After this event the Ch'ŏyong mask was used by the people for exorcising demons. Views differ as to the origin of Ch'ŏyong, but it is safe to consider his dance a dance of folk origin dating from the ninth century. The thirteenth-century text of the choral dance of Ch'ŏyong attests to the popularity of Ch'ŏyong and his power in the Koryŏ period. In the early fifteenth century, this dance was thoroughly revised by King Sejong as the most important court dance in the Yi dynasty. Together with other court dances, it was performed at court on New Year's Eve, at the fifth watch (see chap. ii).[2]

Puzzling yet characteristic mask dances in Silla are the "Five Shows" *(ogi)*, as recorded in Ch'oe Ch'i-wŏn's poems. They are, in the Korean reading of the logographs, the *kŭmhwan*, *wŏlchŏn* (from Khotan), *taemyŏn*, *soktok* (from Sogdiana), and *sanye* and are thought all to be of Central Asian origin.

The most famous mask play in Korea is *sandae*, which originated toward the end of Koryŏ.[3] It was performed on a stage by masked actors following a script which presents a story with spoken lines and intermittent dances and songs. The *sandae* was further developed in the fifteenth century, when it became one of the important official observances of the Yi dynasty. The court protected and encouraged this play in order to present it before the Chinese envoy as a chief entertainment upon his arrival in Korea on yearly official missions. Actors and musicians gathered together on this occasion, and the foreign dignitaries were entertained at the outskirts of Seoul just before they entered the capital. The *sandae*, under court auspices, became the repository of all mask plays of folk origin; it even incorporated the Ch'ŏyong dance as well as the *narye*[4] of Koryŏ.

The play opens with a shamanist offering to the spirits of the land, and consists of ten scenes or acts, each named for a character in that act, such as "The High Priest," "The Pock-Marked Priest," "The Dark-Faced Priest," "The Priest of the Blinking Eyes," and the like. As in the *Kkoktukaksi* puppet

---

[2]The particulars of this elaborate ritual are recorded in the section on "Hangnyŏnhwadae Ch'ŏyongmu hapsŏl" in the *Akhak kwebŏm* ("Canon of Music," 1493), V, 11b-16a.

[3]Also called *sandae togam kŭk*. The word *sandae* (or *sandi*) has been studied by scholars, but no one knows its origin or meaning. The *sandae*, as we have it today, originated in Kyŏnggi province: *pon sandae* in the western suburbs of Seoul, and *pyŏl* (or *Yangju*) *sandae* in the old village of Yanju. *Pon sandae*, however, disappeared, and only *pyŏl sandae* survives today.

[4]A court ceremony held on New Year's Eve to exorcise evil spirits.

play, the theme is the triangular affair of a yangban, his wife, and his concubine. The play, in its later version, pours scorn upon the Yi nobility as well as on the apostate priests. The *sandae* has an all-male cast, and its performance is accompanied by drums, strings, and brass instruments. Besides official occasions, it was performed on a makeshift stage in open air in the village square on festival occasions such as on the eighth day of the fourth moon, the fifth day of the fifth moon, and the fifteenth day of the eighth moon. The *sandae* still survives today.

The *Haesŏ* (also called Pongsan mask dance) and *Hahoe*[5] are other representative mask plays originating from Hwanghae and North Kyŏngsang provinces respectively. In the *Haesŏ*,[6] a seven-act play, the roles vary slightly according to the locality in which it is performed. It is presented in the village square, without a stage, and at the conclusion the masks and costumes are thrown into a bonfire in the belief that they are possessed of evil spirits. The *Hahoe,* a five-act play, is presented as part of a shamanist service intended to cleanse the village of evil spirits. It is performed on the second and fifteenth days of the first lunar month in honor of two female tutelary deities who are worshipped annually, although the mask play is performed only in a large-scale decennial ceremony. The moderator of the ceremony, usually a village elder, after observing a ritual fast and purification, opens the box containing the masks. Sixteen male actors and musicians, chosen among the villagers, then proceed to the altar on the hilltop, make offerings, and perform a dance. The same dance is repeated on the fifteenth day to mark the end of the ceremony. The masks, mostly reddish in color, are carved from sandalwood and have holes pierced for the eyes and mouth. Some have the lower jaw separate and tied on with strings, in order to give a more realistic appearance. The fourth act, a mime, portrays a lion fighting and is said to symbolize an exorcism to ward off evil spirits and to welcome good luck for the new year.

In both the *Haesŏ* and *Hahoe* there are bitter attacks on the bureaucracy, Buddhist clergy, and shamans and on current fashions of thought and behavior.

The Kkoktukaksi (or *Pak ch'ŏmji*), the representative Korean puppet play, is presented by an itinerant troupe of six or seven members, three of whom are usually musicians. The puppet dramatis personae consist of Pak Ch'ŏmji (the hero), his wife (Kkoktukaksi), his concubine (Tolmorijip), his younger brother

[5]The name of a village in North Kyŏngsang.

[6]Unlike other mask plays which generally lack a sense of unity, the *Pongsan* has a simple yet ordered structure. (1) The apostate monk Ch'wibal, who has been enticed by a devil to tempt an old master of the Law, orders four head monks to dance in front of a temple where the master is reciting the *Diamond Sūtra;* (2) Through the manipulation of Ch'wibal eight monks break their vows and dance before the master in order to corrupt him; (3) An itinerant dancing girl swirls around before the master in another attempt to deprave him; (4) Ch'wibal, two female shamans, eight monks, and the master dance together, suggesting that the master has finally fallen from grace; (5) A lion is dispatched by the Buddha to punish Ch'wibal and his companions for leading the master astray. When the fierce animal devours one of the monks, the others come to their senses, promise to repent, and dance with the lion; (6) Malttuk, a nobleman's servant, caricatures a corrupt official and arrests Ch'wibal. The seventh scene, which is perhaps a later addition, virtually unrelated to the previous parts of the play, depicts a conflict between a female shaman and her lover.

(So Pak Ch'ŏmji), two young Shaman priestesses, and others. There are, in addition, a dog, pheasant, falcon, and snake. Musicians are included in the cast as villagers. It has eight acts, each independent of the others.

Realistic rather than symbolic, the puppets adhere to the text closely. But the length of the performance depends entirely on the circumstances and the interpretation of the narrators. Often several acts are omitted, but the main plot is always presented. As in the *sandae,* the object of exaggerated humor and satire is the yangban class (Acts V, VI, VII) and priests (II, VIII). When the troupe was invited by nobles, Act VII was omitted because of its open attack on the Yi bureaucracy.

Drama in Korea was essentially a folk art. It grew among, and was a property of, the common people. The mask and puppet plays, as we have seen, were closely associated with the shamanist and Buddhist religions, the folk songs and dances formed the basis of the plays. The texts have little literary merit. No drama text survives from the times of Silla and Koryŏ, except fragments of choral songs used perhaps in a mask play.

The drama, which could have developed into a literary genre, was denied its development owing to the conditions of Yi society. Actors occupied the lowest of the lower social strata, and no serious writer was interested in writing a play for his inferiors. The only form in which popular plays could survive was in occasional entertainments at court or at noble houses or at fairs and festivals. Actors therefore had to tour the country after the harvest, during the farmers' leisure season, barely subsisting on donations or villagers' good-will.

In addition to mask and puppet plays, there was another kind of dramatic entertainment in Korea, the *p'ansori.*[7] Like the minstrel in medieval Europe, the *kwangdae* was a professional entertainer who recreated, dramatized, and sang known tales and narratives. What he did was select the most dramatic episodes from oral tradition and sing them with gestures and to the accompaniment of a drum. The first recorded singers of the *p'ansori* were Ha Han-dam and Ch'oe Sŏn-dal in the beginning of the eighteenth century. The *p'ansori* developed in the southwestern part of Korea, chiefly in Chŏlla province. The singers wrote the texts and composed the tunes, and their repertory consisted of twelve titles *(madang).* Among them the most famous was the *Ch'unhyang chŏn.*

Many popular novels such as the *Ch'unhyang chŏn, Simch'ŏng chŏn,* and *Sugyŏng nangja chŏn* ("Story of Sugyŏng") were outgrowths of the *p'ansori,* demonstrating their origin unmistakably in their style; they were meant to be recited or sung rather than read. The texts of the *p'ansori* differed from ordinary novels in that they were sung outdoors for the immediate audience who gathered there to enjoy the performer's vocal talents as well as his narrative skill. Another characteristic of popular *p'ansori* was the incorporation of popu-

---

[7]Like *sandae, p'ansori* is a debated term whose origin and meaning are unknown.

lar folk songs. The *Ch'unhyang chŏn*, for instance, contains thirty-six songs of folk origin. In the nineteenth century, Sin Chae-hyo (1812-1884), the most famous writer of *p'ansori*, revised six of the twelve traditional titles in the repertory. Today the *p'ansori* is no longer a popular art.

Bibliography: the *Drama*

Chang Sa-hun, *Kugak kaeyo* ("Outline of Korean Music") (1961).
Cho Yun-je, *Kungmunhak kaesŏl* (1960), 208-236.
——————————, *Hanguk munhak sa* (1963), pp. 378-385.
Ch'oe Sang-su, *Annual Customs of Korea* (1960).
——————————, *Hahoe kamyŏn'gŭk ŭi yŏn'gu* ("A Study of the Mask Play of Hahoe") (1959).
Chŏng No-sik, *Chosŏn ch'anggŭk sa* ("History of Korean Ch'anggŭk") (1940).
Ham Hwa-jin, *Chosŏn ŭmak t'ongnon* ("Outline of Korean Music") (1948).
Kim Chae-ch'ŏl, *Chosŏn yŏn'gŭk sa* ("History of Korean Drama") (1933).
Song Sŏk-ha, *Hanguk minsok ko* ("Studies in Korean Folklore") (1960).
Yi Hye-gu, *Hanguk ŭmak yŏn'gu* ("Studies in Korean Music") (1957).
Yi Pyŏng-gi, *Kungmunhak kaeron* ("Outline of Korean Literature") (1961), pp. 81-99, 149-173.

. . .

Chang Chu-gŭn, "Chejudo muga" ("Shamanist Songs on Cheju Island"), *KK*, 19 (1958), 150-167.
Ch'oe Sang-su, "Hanguk min'gan chŏnsŭng yuhŭi chi" ("Popular Games in Korea"), *MH*, 2 (1957), 129-197.
——————————, "Hanguk sŏbu ŭi kamyŏn mugŭk" ("Mask Dance Play in Southern Korea"), *MH*, 1 (1956), 76-81.
——————————, *"Kkoktukaksi* inhyŏnggŭk ŭi yŏn'gu" ("A Study of the Puppet Play"), *MH*, 1 (1956), 20-75.
——————————, *"Ogwandae* yayu kamyŏn'gŭk haeje" ("Introduction to the *Ogwandae")* MH, 2 (1957), 256-280.
——————————, *"Paebaengikut taesa"* ("The Text of the *Paebaengikut"), MH*, 1 (1956), 180-188; 2 (1957), 201-226, 228-255.
Ch'oe Ŭng-nok, *"Kasa* munhaksange nat'anan sesi p'ungsok koch'al" ("Korean Customs as They Appear in *Kasa* Literature"), *Chŏnnam University Kungmunhak po*, 3 (1962), 44-94.
Cho Wŏn-gyŏng, "Narye wa kamyŏn mugŭk" ("Exorcism and Mask Dance Play"), *Hangnim* (Yŏnse Univ.), 4 (1955), 16-89.
Im Sŏk-chae "Kangnyŏng t'alch'um taesa" ("Text of Kangnyŏng Mask Dance"), *HM*, III/5 (1957), 285-299.
Kang Kwŏn, "Hanguk inhyŏnggŭk sogo" ("A Study of Korean Puppet Play"), *KK*, 16 (1957), 112-122.
Kim Sa-yŏp, "Chapkihŭi ko" ("A Study of Various Sports and Plays in Korea"), *YHS*, pp. 139-172.
Kim T'aek-kyu, *"Yŏnggo ko"* ("A Study of *Yŏnggo")*, *KKY*, 2 (1958), 5-16.
Son Chin-t'ae, ed., *"Sŏngin nori p'unyŏm* kwa *myŏngnori p'unyŏm"* ("*Sŏngin nori p'unyŏm* and *myŏngnori p'unyŏm"*), *Sajo*, 1 (1958), 242-254.

Yang Chae-yŏn, "Hwahŭi ("Fire Festival"), *CTN,* III (1958), 73-92.
_____, "Kŏmmuhŭi" ("Sword Dance"), *YHS,* pp. 343-359.
_____, *"Muae*-hŭi sogo" ("A Note on *Muae"), Mun'gyŏng,* 1 (1955), 7-12.
_____, *"Sandae*-hŭi e ch'wihayŏ" ("On the *Sandae* Mask Play"), in *Thirtieth Anniversary Volume of Chungang University,* pp. 189-212.
Ye Yong-hae, ed., *In'gan munhwajae* ("Masters of Cultural Heritage") (1963), pp. 15-18, 55-187.
Yi Tu-hyŏn, "Hanguk ŭi kamyŏn" ("Korean Masks"), *Sajo,* I/5 (1958), 238-244.
_____, "Sandae togam kŭk ŭi sŏngnip e taehayŏ" ("On the Formation of the *Sandae* Mask Play"), *KK,* 18 (1957), 9-41.
_____, "Silla ogi ko" ("On the 'Five Shows' of Silla"), *STN,* IX (1959), 183-208.
Yu Han-sang, "Hahoe pyŏlsin kamyŏn mugok taesa" ("Texts of the *Hahoe* Mask Play"), *KK,* 20 (1959), 191-198.

                                                                 P'ansori
Kim Tong-uk, *"P'ansori* palsaeng ko" ("The Origins of *P'ansori"), STN,* II (1955), 167-205; III (1956), 239-301.
_____, *"P'ansori* sabip kayo rŭl wihan siron" ("On the Interposed Songs in *P'ansori"), STN,* VII (1958), 245-309.
Sin Chae-hyo, *Sin Chae-hyo chŏnjip,* ed. Kang Han-yŏng (4 vols.; 1962-)
Son Nak-pŏm, "Sin Chae-hyo wa *Pyŏn'gangsoe chŏn"* (Sin Chae-hyo and *Pyŏn'gangsoe chŏn"), Haksulgye,* 1 (1958), 55-61.
Yi Pyŏng-gi, ed., *Karujigi t'aryŏng* (1949).

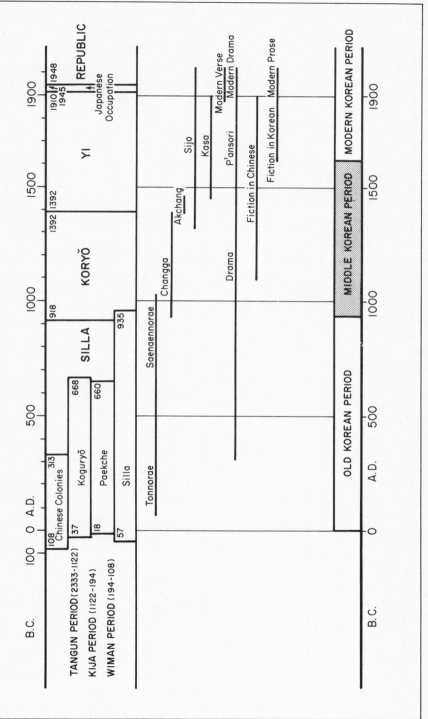

Development of Vernacular Genres of Prose and Verse in Korea

X. Writings in Chinese

Because of geographical proximity, the importation of Chinese characters and classics into the ancient Korean kingdoms must have taken place as early as the second century before Christ. The fact of cultural intercourse between China and the Korean states is documented by Chinese sources which attest to the two-way traffic in early days. We have such titles of early compositions as the *Hwangjo ka* ("Song of Yellow Birds"), by King Yuri, and *Konghuin* ("Melody for Harp"),[1] by Yŏok, whose authenticity is suspect. With the establishment of the Chinese commanderies in the peninsula, the flow of Chinese culture rapidly increased, and Koguryŏ, which rose from the territories of one of those commanderies, had contacts with Chinese immigrants there and used Chinese characters long before it became a kingdom. The inscription on the monument erected in honor of King Kwanggaet'o (391-412), consisting of 1,759 characters, is an example of the literary accomplishment of the Koguryŏ people. In 600 Yi Mun-jin compiled an official history of Koguryŏ, and in 612 General Ŭlchi Mundŏk wrote a five-word *chüeh-chü* to overawe the enemy general, Yü Chung-wen, on the occasion of Sui's invasion. Chinese was freely used in diplomatic and official documents in Paekche from the middle of the fourth century. An official history was compiled in the time of King Kŭnch'ogo (346-375); in 472 a royal message was sent to Northern Wei, and in 541 an envoy was sent to Liang requesting commentaries on the *Nirvāṇa Sūtra* and the *Book of Songs*. Even in Silla, which received continental culture much later than Koguryŏ and Paekche, Chinese was an official written language from the time of King Naemul (356-401). During the reign of Kings Pŏphŭng and Chijŭng the use of Chinese increased, and in 545 King Chinhŭng ordered Kŏch'ilbu to compile a national history. The inscriptions on King Chinhŭng's monuments erected at the sites of his royal inspections are good pieces of writing in Chinese.

After the unification of the peninsula, Chinese learning developed further in Silla. In 651 the national university was established, and students devoted nine years of study to the *Analects, Book of Filial Piety, Book of Changes, Collected Ritual,* and the like. Great scholars came one after another: Kang Su

---

[1]See *Ku-chin chu (Han-Wei ts'ung-shu* 15), II, 2a-b.

(c. 654-692), who excelled in composing diplomatic documents; Sŏl Ch'ong (b. 655), who systematized the *idu* letters; and Kim Tae-mun whose now unavailable *Hwarang segi, Akpon,* and *Hansan ki* furnished Kim Pu-sik with invaluable data for the history of the three kingdoms. But the one who brought Chinese learning to completion in Silla was Ch'oe Ch'i-wŏn (857-915), who passed the civil service examination at the T'ang court at the age of eighteen. There he wrote the famous manifesto on the occasion of the rebellion of Huang Ch'ao and returned to Korea in 885. Altogether, fifty-eight Silla nationals passed the T'ang examination, and they studied chiefly T'ang poetry and parallel prose. The use of the *Wen hsüan* ("Anthology of Literature") in the Silla university as a textbook must have furthered the use of parallel prose among scholars and writers.

With the establishment of the national university in Koryŏ in 930 and the system of the civil service examination from 958, Chinese became the medium of expression among the literati. The adoption of the examination system encouraged the candidates to study only Chinese classics, histories, and belles-lettres and emphasized scholarly and literary skills. Therefore, men of literary talent started to worship China and to neglect the indigenous culture which they had inherited from the previous dynasty. The parallel prose style continued to be practised in early Koryŏ, but from the time of King Sŏngjong (1049-1083-1094), it began to yield its supremacy to pre-Han and Han styles. This change in stylistics was also reflected in the university, where the *Wen hsüan* was no more on the regular curriculum. Even so, in the beginning of the twelfth century a Sung envoy to Koryŏ noted the lingering effect of parallel prose in Korean writing. Ch'oe Ch'ung (984-1068), who established the first private institution of learning in Koryŏ, and Pak Il-lyang still wrote in parallel prose. But Kim Pu-sik (1075-1151), author of the *Samguk sagi,* definitely advocated reform in prose style.

After the *coup d'état* by the military class in 1170, scholar-statesmen lost their political prestige and hid themselves in remote mountains and villages. There they taught children of the literati class and bequeathed their literary tradition to such writers of the twelfth and thirteenth centuries as Yi In-no, Im Ch'un, Yi Kyu-bo, Chin Hwa, and Ch'oe Cha. Yi In-no, author of the *P'ahan chip* ("Gleanings from Leisure Hours"), wrote crystal-pure and elegant verse. Yi Kyu-bo sang fondly of such plants and animals as the duckweed, heron, and sea anemone, and his poetic spring was so nearly inexhaustible that he even composed in dreams. He was praised for his originality and for the transcendental quality in his verse and was compared to Li Po in his lifetime. His preferred poet was Po Chü-i, and his middle and later poems show his indebtedness to this Chinese master. His prose was as significant as his poetry. He was deeply versed in Taoism and Buddhism, especially the Zen and T'ien-t'ai sects, and drew freely from these two teachings to enrich his writing.

In the beginning of the fourteenth century Neo-Confucianism was imported to Korea by An Hyang (1243-1306) or by Paek I-jŏng (fl. 1314). Scholars soon turned to Neo-Confucianism, rejected Buddhism, and preached that the study of the classics should come before that of belles-lettres. Great names during this period are Yi Che-hyŏn, Yi Saek, and Chŏng Mong-ju. Yi Che-hyŏn went several times to the Yüan court on diplomatic missions, and his fame was widespread in literary circles there. He was the first to master the *tz'u* form of verse, which he used in some of his best poems. The verse of Yi Saek was characterized by majestic lines. He taught Chu Hsi's philosophy at court and cultivated men of ability who were to carry his learning over to the Yi dynasty. Chŏng Mong-ju, perhaps the greatest student of Neo-Confucianism, was credited with being the father of that philosophy in Korea.

The Koryŏ dynasty also produced a host of priest-poets, Sŏnt'an, Ch'ŏnin, Chinjŏng (d. 1130), and Iryŏn. Among important works which are still extant are: the *Kyunyŏ Chŏn* (1075), *Samguk sagi* (1146), *Haedong kosŭng chŏn* ("Lives of Eminent Korean Monks," 1215), *Samguk yusa* (c. 1285), and *Chewang un'gi* ("Rhymed History of Emperors and Kings," 1287).

Meritorious subjects who assisted Yi Sŏng-gye in founding the Yi dynasty were literary men versed in the teachings of Neo-Confucianism. Among them the most noteworthy were Chŏng To-jŏn and Kwŏn Kŭn, who rejected Buddhism as a heterodox religion and instituted Sung rationalism as the official political philosophy of the new dynasty. The Neo-Confucianism which they accepted as a guiding ideology emphasized metaphysics, in particular the theory of the five relations and its application in social, political, and ethical spheres. Henceforth all political and cultural activities were judged and standardized by the yardstick of this new philosophy. As a result of such dogmatism, the development of native sensibility and creativity in the arts was stifled.

Within thirty years of the founding of the Yi, Neo-Confucianism came to dominate the Korean world of thought and education. Scholars during this period were mostly those who passed the examination at the end of the Koryŏ dynasty and supported the Yi usurpation: Ha Yun, Kwŏn Kŭn, Pyŏn Kye-ryang, and Yun Hoe. When King Sejong established the Hall of Scholars (see chap. iii) and encouraged learning and literature, a series of learned men gathered under this great king: Sin Suk-chu (1417-1475), Chŏng In-ji (1397-1478), Pak P'aeng-nyŏn (1417-1456), and Sŏng Sam-mun (1418-1456). The greatest writer in the early Yi period was Sŏ Kŏ-jŏng (1420-1488), compiler of the *Samguksa chŏryo* ("Summary of the History of the Three Kingdoms"), *Tongguk t'onggam* ("General Mirror of the Eastern Country"), *Tongin sihwa,* and others. The tendency among these men was to continue to practise the ancient style in prose and to study T'ang poetry and one Sung poet, Huang T'ing-chien (1045-1105).

An important change that took place in the learned world in the sixteenth century was a split between two groups of scholars, one emphasizing philosophy and the other pure literature and literary arts. The former group of scholars were purists who in their aspiration scorned worldly careers and lived far from the court. Earlier, Kil Chae (1353-1419), a surviving Koryŏ loyalist, had set the pattern in the South, in Sŏnsan, where he taught his disciples the Confucian classics, especially the *Lesser Learning*. Kil Chae was a follower of Chŏng Mong-ju in his emphasis on the study of the classics and the actual practice of the sage's teachings. His teaching was bequeathed to Kim Chong-jik (1431-1492), Kim Koeng-p'il (1454-1504), and finally to Cho Kwang-jo (1482-1519). After the usurpation of Sejo in 1455 and the misgovernment by tyrant Yŏnsan'gun, the people were reduced to great misery and ethics and morality were slackened. Upon his enthronement, therefore, King Chungjong realized that Neo-Confucianism, emphasizing the five relations, was the best means of governing his country and people. He himself lectured on the *Great Learning* and clearly outlined the path Yi dynasty scholarship should take. That path was expressed in the following message: "Study of Confucian classics is the root, and the art of literary composition is the branch." And in 1515, with the advent of Cho Kwang-jo, who was known to his generation as a supreme interpreter of the classics and assiduous practitioner of Confucian virtues, the condition of the academic world came to be completely changed.

Cho Kwang-jo introduced reforms into the civil service examination and university curriculum. He and his group advocated a close study of the classics and scorned as "spurious art" the composition of essays and verse which had hitherto been the major part of the examination, asserting that the emphasis on literary skills amounted to a utilitarian exploitation of classical learning, but not of its re-creation or practice in one's own age. Ardent reformists and militant Confucianists who were determined to re-create the age of Yao and Shun in Korea, they condemned practitioners of literary art as "superficial and frivolous," even arguing that the sovereign should not compose poetry and should not command his officials to compose verse for presentation to him. Their radical reform movement was challenged by older officials and scholars who followed the traditional mode of learning in the country. They refuted the charge made against them by Cho's group and pointed out the importance of the literary arts. Thus the world of Chinese learning was divided into two groups, the adherents of textual criticism (philosophy) and those of belles-lettres (literature). Since traditional Chinese learning in Korea had been a mixture of both philosophy and literature, the distinct division between the two meant a new development of pure literature in Chinese. Also since literature became constantly an object of criticism by the philosophy school, writings in Chinese came to have more content and substance. To the literature school belonged Kim Il-son, Nam Kon, Cho Wi, and Nam Hyo-on. The first three were all considered to have been disciples of Kim Chong-jik, who was often considered to be the champion of Neo-Confucianism in the early Yi period but who was actually more skilled in verse and prose than philosophy. Important poets were Pak Ŭn (1479-1504), who died young in the literati purge of 1504;

Yi Haeng (1478-1534), who excelled in the five-word verse; and Sŏng Hyŏn, author of the *Yongjae ch'onghwa* ("Collected Works of Yongjae") and *Akhak kwebŏm*. Important scholars who belonged to the philosophy school were Kim An-guk, Kim Chŏng-guk, No Su-sin (1515-1590), Yi Hwang, and Yi I.

Chinese writings in Korea reached maturity during the reign of King Sŏnjo. A host of major writers adorned the literary world. A group of three poets, Ch'oe Kyŏng-ch'ang (1539-1583), Paek Kwang-hun (1537-1582), and Yi Tal studied chiefly T'ang poets and wrote only verse. In the beginning of the dynasty, Su Tung-p'o was in vogue, but from the middle of the sixteenth century writers turned again to T'ang poetry. The great prose writer of the day was Ch'oe Ip (1539-1612), who was versed in the writings of Ou-yang Hsiu (1007-1070) and practised the ancient style. Ch'a Ch'ŏn-no (1556-1615) is worthy of mention for his masculine style; he also wrote verse, chiefly seven-word *lü-shih* (regulated verse) and five-word verse. Kwŏn P'il (1569-1612) and Yi An-nul (1571-1637) also left jewels in poetry. A group of four writers known in literary history as the "Four Masters" are Yi Chŏng-gu (1564-1635), Sin Hŭm (1566-1628), Chang Yu (1587-1638), and Yi Sik (1584-1647). The writings of Yi Chŏng-gu were well known not only in Korea, but also in China, where they were unanimously praised by the Ming critics for their freshness of imagery and noble emotion. Sin Hŭm, author of the *Sangch'on chip* ("Collected Works of Sangch'on"), was a man of wide learning who excelled in verse. Chang Yu was a versatile poet who tried such Chinese forms as the *sao, fu, tz'u,* and *lü shih*. Leader of the belles-lettres school, he drew freely from Taoism and Buddhism to embellish his prose and verse. Yi Sik, on the other hand, proposed that one should study the *Book of Songs* as well as *Ch'u tz'u* and perfect one's study by following the poems of Tu Fu as one's models. In prose he suggested Han Yü (786-824) as a model.

The more Neo-Confucianism developed, the further became the gap between that Sung rationalism and the everyday life of the people. Sung philosophy, however lucid or profound its theories might be, could not solve the actual problems of the Korean people. The elucidation of the Supreme Ultimate or of *ch'i* and *li*[2] alone could not solve the pressing social and economic needs of the day. As a reaction to this empty idealism which proved itself to be of little use after the Japanese and Manchu invasions, practical learning arose among a handful of learned men. The beginning of practical learning *(sirhak)* in Korea is often identified with Yu Hyŏng-wŏn (1622-1673). Yu made a thorough historical research to analyze the current political system as well as the tax and landholding systems. In his *Pan'gye surok* ("Essays of Pan'gye," 1652-1670; 26 chaps.) he outlined measures for land reform. But the bud of

---

[2]Variously translated as "either," "matter," "element," "material force," "vital force," or "matter energy," in the Neo-Confucian metaphysics of Chu Hsi's school, *ch'i* is a designation for the basic matter or stuff of the universe. *Li* is a designation for the immaterial and metaphysical principles that underlie, yet transcend, the physical universe. See Fung Yu-lan, *A History of Chinese Philosophy*, tr. Derk Bodde (Princeton, 1953), II, 434 ff.

the *sirhak* movement had been visible even in the beginning of the seventeenth century. Yi Su-gwang (1563-1629) and Kim Yuk[3] (1580-1658) actively imported Catholicism and new sciences from Peking. Yi, who went to Peking three times on diplomatic missions, introduced to Korea for the first time European learning from such countries as England and France and elucidated Catholicism. He was also a champion of Korean literature and laid emphasis on the true values of vernacular poetry. Kim Yuk brought from Peking books on the calendar and mathematics, advocated land reform and the minting of coins, and urged the use of the water wheel and other machines to lighten the burden of farmers. Following Yu Hyŏng-wŏn, Yi Ik (1682-1764) not only advocated the well-field system in agriculture but also made historical researches in and textual criticism of the classics in his *Sŏngho sasŏl*.[4] With the coming of Pak Chi-wŏn (1737-1805; see chap. vii), practical learning was not only firmly established, but became the dominant trend of thought.

Pak read widely to discover the best solution for reforming the current administration. His great reform proposal concerned the written language of the day. Idealists blindly following Neo-Confucianism still wrote in the literary language of China, a foreign language and a dead one at that. Pak, on his return from China, wrote the *Yŏrha ilgi* ("Jehol Diary") in a new style drawing freely from the colloquial language spoken in China and used in popular literature such as the novel and the drama. King Chŏngjo, however, was a purist in style and supported the antiquated literary language and termed the *Yŏrha ilgi* "unorthodox". But Pak scorned tradition and continued to write an easy and practical prose that could be understood by men of average education. His masterpiece, the *Kwanong soch'o* ("Handbook of Agriculture"),[5] was written to promote the welfare of the people. By the end of the eighteenth century, he and his disciples — among whom the greatest was Chŏng Yag-yong (1762-1836) — had laid a firm foundation for practical learning and for the new literary style which emphasized spontaneous expression of emotion and originality and freedom in literary works.

The last poet of importance before the fall of the Yi dynasty was Sin Wi (1769-1845), who was skilled in painting, calligraphy, and verse. He was perhaps the most voluminous poet of the Yi period. Like Yi Che-hyŏn, Sin translated the famous *sijo* into Chinese, using the seven-word verse form.

In 1894 the civil service examination was abolished, and official documents began to appear in a mixture of Korean and Chinese. The study of Confucian

---

[3]For Kim's role in the introduction of the tribute tax system see Ching Young Choe, "Kim Yuk (1580-1658) and the Taedongbŏp Reform," *Journal of Asian Studies*, XXIII, No. 1 (1963), 21-35.

[4]This book is a collection of Yi's essays in thirty chapters and is divided into five headings: Heaven and Earth, Creation, Human Affairs, Classics and History, and Verse and Prose. It describes Western theories on astronomy and geography and sets store by the positive methods of historiography. His interpretation of the Tangun myth, for example, is a scientific investigation of the nature of the myth.

[5]The book, consisting of fifteen chapters, deals with agrarian reform and methods and techniques of farming. It was presented to the throne in 1799.

scholarship and philosophy, which had been the only path to success and fame, declined, and writings in Chinese gave way to the rise of a new literature. Writers no longer used Chinese as the literary language, and the age of Confucianism and Neo-Confucianism was over in Korea.

Bibliography: *Writings in Chinese*

Cho Yun-je, *Hanguk munhak sa* (1963), pp. 19-25, 48-57, 68-72, 107-114, 155-159, 184-202, 264-293, 294-304, 385-392.

―――――――――, *Kungmunhak kaesŏl* (1960), pp. 227-245, 427-441.

Kim Sa-yŏp, *Kungmunhak sa* (1956), pp. 109-111, 125-133, 202-220, 296-301, 336-338, 391-403, 454-468, 498-501.

Kim T'ae-jun, *Chosŏn hanmunhak sa* ("History of Chinese Writings in Korea") (1931).

Ku Cha-gyun, *Chosŏn p'yŏngmin munhak sa. I. kŭndae p'yŏngmin hanmunhak sa* ("History of Korean Plebeian Literature. I. Chinese Writings in the Latter Yi Dynasty") (1948).

Yi Ka-wŏn, *Hanguk hanmunhak sa* ("History of Chinese Writings in Korea") (1961).

Yu Hong-nyŏl, *Kojong ch'iha ŭi Sŏhak sunan ŭi yŏn'gu* ("Tne Persecution of Western Learning under King Kojong") (1962).

· · ·

Bibliography Compilation Committee, ed., *Hanguk yŏktae myŏngsi chŏnsŏ* ("Anthology of Famous Chinese Verses in Korea") (1959).

Ch'ungnam University, tr., *Kugyŏk chuhae Pan'gye surok* ("Essays of Pan'gye; An Annotated Translation [of chaps. 9-12]") (1962).

Kim Ki-dong and Im Hong-do, eds., *Hanmun sosŏl sŏnjip* ("Anthology of Fiction in Chinese") (1960).

Korean Classics Translation Committee, tr., *Kugyŏk Yulgok sŏngrihak chŏnsŏ* ("Neo-Confucian Writings of Yulgok: An Annotated Translation") (1961).

The Research Division of the Agricultural Bank, tr. and ed., *Kugyŏk Pan'gye surok* ("Essays of Pan'gye on the Landholding System: A Translation") (1959).

Wŏn Ch'ang-gyu, tr., *Wanyŏk Mongmin simsŏ* ("Complete Translation of the *Mongmin simsŏ*") (1962).

Yi Ka-wŏn, tr., *Yijo hanmun sosŏl sŏn* ("Anthology of Yi Dynasty Fiction in Chinese") (1961).

Yulgok Commemoration Committee, tr., *Kugŏk Yulgok chŏnsŏ chŏngsŏn* ("Selected Translations from the Essays of Yulgok") (1957).

. . .
Han U-gŭn, "Sŏngho Yi Ik yŏn'gu" ("A Study of Yi Ik"), *CH*, 20 (1959), 7-78.
_____,"Yijo sirhak ŭi kaenyŏm e taehayŏ" ("On the Nature of 'Practical Learning' in the Yi Dynasty"), *CH*, 19 (1958), 25-46.
Hong I-sŏp, *Chŏng Yag-yong ŭi chŏngch'i kyŏngje sasang yŏn'gu* ("Studies in the Political and Economic Thought of Chŏng Yag-yong") (1959).
Im Ch'ang-sun, "Im Il-gwi wa kŭ haksŏl: Hanguk yuhaksa ŭi iltanmyŏn" ("Im Il-gwi and His Theories: His Place in the History of Korean Confucianism"), *SGTN*, III (1958), 151-164.
Ko Pyŏng-ik, "Hyech'o *Wang och'ŏnch'ukkuk* yŏn'gu saryak" ("A History of Studies on Hyech'o's 'Record of the Pilgrimage to the Five Countries'), *PPN*, pp. 299-316.
Pang Chong-hyŏn "Tok *Kŭnjae chip* hu" ("Upon Reading the *Kŭnjae chip*"), *HG*, 107 (1949), 35-42.
_____, "Tok *T'aech'on chip* hu" ("Upon Reading the *T'aech'on chip*"), *HG*, 101 (1947), 2-8.
Sin Ki-hyŏng, "Yŏnam ŭi sirhak sasang" ("Yŏnam's Theories on 'Practical Learning'"), *Mun'gyŏng*, 4 (1957), 81-101.
Sŏ Su-saeng, "Tongguk munjong Ch'oe Koun ŭi munhak" ("The Works of Ch'oe Ch'iwŏn, Master of Chinese Writings in Korea"), *Ŏmunhak*, 1 (1956), 81-88; 2 (1958), 63-93.
Yi Ka-wŏn, Hanmun munch'e ŭi pullyujŏk yŏn'gu" ("The Stylistic Classification cf Chinese Writings"), *AY*, III/1 (1960), 129-168; III/2 (1960), 159-192.
_____, "Sŏkpuk munhak yŏn'gu" ("A Study of the Works of Sŏkpuk [Sin Kwang-su, 1712-1775]"), *TH*, IV (1959), 149-204.
Yi Kyu-bo, *"Tongmyŏng wang"* ("King Tongmyŏng"), tr. Yang Chae-yŏn, *HM*, I /10 (1955), 235-241.
Yi U-sŏng, "Sirhakp'a ŭi munhak: Pak Yŏnam ŭi kyŏngu" ("The Writings of Upholders of Practical Learning: The Case of Pak Yŏnam"), *KK*, 16 (1957), 84-100.
Yi Ŭr-ho, "Yubul sanggyo e myŏn esŏ pon Chŏng Tasan" ("Chŏng Tasan Seen from the Confucian and Buddhist Viewpoints"), *PPN*, pp. 7 05-730.
Yun Wŏn-ho, "Hanguk sup'il ŭi p'yŏnmo: Koryŏ Yijo sup'il ŭl chungsim ŭro" ("An Aspect of Essays in Korea, Especially in the Koryŏ and Yi Dynasties"), *YHS*, pp. 379-391.

Translations

Fuchs, Walter, "Huei-ch'ao's Pilgerreise durch Nordwest-Indien und Zentral-Asien um 726," *Sitzungsberichte der Preussischen Akademie der Wissenschaften*, Philosophisch-historische Klasse (Berlin, 1939), pp. 426-469.
Lee, Peter H., "The Life of the Korean Poet-Priest Kyunyŏ," *Asiatische Studien/ Etudes Asiatiques*, XI, Nos. 1-2 (1957-1958), 42-72.
_____, *Lives of Eminent Korean Monks (1215)*, [forthcoming]
Szczesniak, Boleslaw, "The Kōtaio [Kwanggaet'o wang] Monument," *Monumenta Nipponica*, VII (1951), 242-268.
Vos, Frits, "Kim Yusin, Persönlichkeit und Mythos," *Oriens Extremus*, I (1954), 29-70; II (1955), 210-236.

TWENTIETH-CENTURY LITERATURE: VERSE AND PROSE

XI. Twentieth-Century Literature: Verse

Modern literature represents nearly a total break with the Korean past. As in China and Japan, a specifically modern type of expression developed much later than in Europe. Not until the beginning of the twentieth century did it make its appearance and, unlike European modern literatures which continued the literary traditions of their own past, it tended to accept and imitate foreign examples. A rapid succession of literary movements and ideas in the short span of fifty years brought confusion to the literary world.

Despite the slowness of its start, Korean modern literature might have borne finer fruit if allowed to mature in a sympathetic and free atmosphere. The buds of the new literature were, however, soon nipped by an unseasonable frost when Korea lost her independence through Japanese occupation in 1905 and annexation in 1910. During the period of thirty-six years from the annexation to the end of the Second World War, the new literature was forced to grow in the shadow of Japanese colonialism. It was doomed to be the literature of an exploited people. Denied the spirit of freedom and dynamism, the new literature in Korea became one of sorrow, reflecting a grief-stricken and despondent outlook. Without the indomitable spirit of the Korean people, Korean literature by itself could neither have preserved the Korean language, which embodies and manifests Korean tradition and culture, nor revealed the ultimate quality of the Korean sensibility. It was a triumph of the Korean spirit that it preserved and continued the Korean language despite Japanese oppression.

The period of 1880-1905 is characterized by the introduction of Western learning and the translating of works of European literature into Korean. Writers felt the urgency of enlightenment and reform; they were anxious to cast off authoritarianism and the evils accompanying it and to inspire an awareness of what it meant to be Koreans. The first novel to express these ideas was written by Yi In-jik (1862-1916). Publication of the *Hyŏl ŭi nu* ("Tears of Blood," 1906) was therefore a turning point in the history of literature, the beginning of a new epoch in Korea.

The next ten years, which may be termed the pioneering period, produced two great men of letters, Ch'oe Nam-sŏn and Yi Kwang-su. The former founded the first literary monthly in Korea, the *Sonyŏn* ("Children," 1908-1911). The new poetry movement may be said to have started with the publication of "From the Sea to Children" and three other poems by Ch'oe in the first number of this magazine. Let me quote "From the Sea to Children":

> The sea—a soaring mountain—
> Lashes and crushes mighty cliffs of rock.
> Those flimsy things, what are they to me?
> "Know ye my power?" The sea lashes
> Threateningly, it breaks, it crushes.
>
> No fear assaults, no terror
> Masters me. Earth's power and pride
> Are tedious toys to me. All that the earth
> Imagines mighty is to me no more
> Than a mere feather floating by.
>
> Who has not bowed his head
> Before my sovereignty, let him come forth.
> Princes of earth, challenge me if you will.
> First Emperor, Napoleon, are you my adversary?
> Come, come then, compete with me.
>
> Perched on a small hill or possessed
> Of an islet or a patch of land,
> Thinking that you alone reign supreme
> In that kingdom small as a grain,
> Approach me, coward, gaze on me.
>
> Only the arching vault of sky, my kin,
> Can equal me, only the vast sky,
> Whose bright image my waters beat.
> Free from sin, free from stain
> It ignores earth's little multitudes.
>
> I scorn the world's madness,
> The overweaning men who seek to use me.
> My love (brave children)—that is given
> Only to those who come to me with love.
> Come, children, let me kiss you and embrace you.

This poem may appear conventional and verbose today, but it retains its place in the history of Korean poetry as the first poem in free verse, written in simple, colloquial language. Yi Kwang-su, justly called the father of modern Korean literature, was the first author to produce the novel of modern consciousness. His characters are enlightened pioneers who long for the new science and civilization and who advocate marriages for love instead of the normal arranged alliances. This longing for modernity for its own sake was soon to be replaced by liberalism and humanism. Both Ch'oe and Yi were in the forefront of the patriotic movement before and after 1910; Ch'oe wrote the celebrated "Declaration of Independence" which kindled hope in millions of souls all over the country on March 1, 1919, the first day of the demonstrations that inaugurated the independence movement.

Shortly before the unsuccessful and costly movement for liberation, Korean students studying in Tokyo, influenced by both European literature and the new Japanese literature, published the magazine *Ch'angjo* ("Creation") in February, 1919. This publication's intent was to advocate national consciousness and to promote the development of new literature. It showed how far the new literary movement had progressed, and it represented a further step in the perfection of a vigorous new literary style. Two other important journals followed *Ch'angjo: P'yehŏ* ("Ruins")[1] in July, 1920, and *Paekcho* ("White Tide") in January, 1922. In this period of experimentation the theories of new poetry were put into practice. Poets, keenly aware of the modern spirit, fostered in the backward literary world of Korea European literary movements which were not contemporary ones but those of the previous century. The poets, having rejected their own traditions and being unable to invent new conventions or a rational structure, were forced to resurrect past European movements and literary theories in order to find conventions which would give coherence and meaning to their otherwise confused experiences and practices. But Western ideas transplanted in such foreign soil could not bear fruit. The *P'yehŏ* school was decadent, and the *Paekcho* school excessively "romantic." Their techniques were Symbolist, but their themes dated back to the advocates of "art for art's sake." *Paekcho* poetry suffered from undue sentimentalism and an emphasis on dream worlds and death. The favorite time was twilight or night, and the setting was usually the bedroom or tomb. The decadence in this poetry reflects the hopeless conditions in Korea after the collapse of the independence movement. The only way open to the poet was flight into the world of the imagination, where he could indulge freely in aimless revery and despair. Isolated and exiled, each spoke his private language and each had his own techniques. Each struggled to find a new mode of expression and a new set of images and symbols adequate for his unrestrained and escapist imagination. A contemporary of these groups, Kim Sowŏl (1903-1934), was a poet of nature and folk tradition, whose work was rich in local color. He sang of the rhythm and transience of nature. His poems unfortunately defy translation, for their effectiveness depends on the simplicity, directness, and intensity of the phrasing. A suggestion of their character may be found in the *Chindallaekkot* ("The Azalea").

---

[1]The magazine's title is said to have been inspired by Schiller's poem. The lines that might have been appropriate for the purpose are from *Das Ideal und Das Leben:* "Monde wechseln, und Geschlechter fliehen,/Ihrer Götterjugend blühen / Wandellos in ewigen Ruin."

You're sick and tired of me.
When you go
I'll bid you goodbye without saying a word.

I'll gather
azaleas on Yak Mountain,
the burning azaleas of Yŏngbyŏn,
and strew them in your path.

Tread gently, please,
step by step, softly,
on the flowers of dedication.

You're sick and tired of me.
When you leave
I'll not weep though I die.

His vitality and sensitiveness rose to fullness of poetry in the *Ch'ohon* ("Incantation"), which makes an impassioned appeal to the soul of his lady to return.

O name broken piecemeal,
strewn in the empty void.
Nameless name, deaf and dumb,
that suffers me to die as I call it.

The last word carved in my heart
was never spoken in the end.
O you that I love,
O you that I love.

Crimson sun hangs on the west peak,
the deer bell and call sadly.
There on the sheer steep peak
I call, call your empty name.

Until sorrow chokes me and unmans me,
still I will call your name.
My voice goes aslant rejected,
lost between heaven and earth.

Were I to become a stone,
I would die calling your name.
O you that I love,
O you that I love.

While the poets oscillated between the worlds of dream and despair, proletarian literature made headway. Between 1924 and 1933 leftist literature flourished in Korea. The Korean Artist Proletariat Federation *(Chosŏn p'ŭro [let'aria] yesul tongmaeng)* was organized in May, 1925. This group of writers proposed to use literature as a means of gaining political objectives. They emphasized the importance of propaganda, and their work dealt exclusively with the proletariat class. Their influence increased when two organs of theirs started to appear in 1926 and 1927. But because they emphasized content more than form, ideology was glorified at the expense of art. As a reaction to their radicalism, which ignored national traditions and disowned Korean life and thought, the movement for national literature, headed by Yang Chu-dong (b. 1903), was founded in 1926. Its purpose was to inspire the development of a national literature which would continue Korean traditions and to purify and enrich the Korean language. The novel, too, borrowed fresh inspiration from the past, and showed revived interest in historical persons and incidents. Students were sent to distant villages to educate the public and to inspire nationalism. At about the same time was formed the Research Association for Occidental Literature which began to campaign against the leftist theories of art and paved the way for the growth of pure poetry.

Meanwhile the chain of opposition tightened. The Proletariat Federation was dissolved by the Japanese police in 1935. On the other hand, general unrest grew among the literati after the Japanese invasion of Manchuria in September, 1931, and the rise of Nazism. As the pressure of Japanese censorship and colonial policies intensified, it became impossible for writers to express themselves freely. They were forced to become invisible, hiding their personalities and convictions behind their works of art. The only territory left for them to explore was the domain of pure poetry, which could transcend the steady aggravation of their situation. Poets found solace in the aestheticism of the 1890's and the perfection of techniques, remote from politics, philosophy, and the problems of society. Two poets of very different natures towered above their fellow writers: Chŏng Chi-yong (b. 1903) and Kim Ki-rim (b. 1909), landmarks of the generation of the thirties. Chŏng, perhaps the best modern poet, has inspired even to this day a host of imitators and followers. His was a poetry of sensuous beauty, marked by a flawless diction and freshness of imagery which have seldom been surpassed. Some of his best poems depend for effect on the skillful use of onomatopoetic expressions, which, if translated, lose their original charm and force. When he embraced Catholicism, his craftsmanship permitted him to produce the best Korean religious poetry of this century. A collection of his later poems, *Paengnoktam* ("The White Deer Lake," 1941), contains some of the jewels of modern poetry. Here the Korean language has met its master, and can reveal its hidden potentialities to the fullest. Every word is precisely right, and every poem reveals a world which the reader has never known or even sensed before. Here the poet, singing of the hills and waters, leads the reader to the harmonious world of nature.

But not all poets of the thirties were of Chŏng's tribe. Some still suffered from the *fin-de-siècle* pangs. Others became lost in the forest of symbols, fondly explored the subconscious, or strode on the "indivisible flux" of consciousness. All in all, the garden of poetry was full of green carnations. In this moment, a school of "intellectualists" headed by Kim Ki-rim, the second important poet of the period, resolved to set the garden in order. They found inspiration and support in the works of Pound, Eliot, Auden, and Spender. In order to replace the twilit dreamy world with concrete images, they first practiced imagist poetry; later, in order to remedy their looseness of techniques, this school, echoing Eliot, advocated the depersonalization of poetry. To illustrate the virtues of organization and accurate language, the "intellectualists" also wrote satirical verse, which purported to be a diagnosis of the unhealthy state of contemporary poetry. In criticism the school hailed clarity and craftsmanship above all, condemned irrationality and sentiment in poetry, and asserted that objectivity and analysis should be the sole criteria of criticism.

With the outbreak of the Sino-Japanese war in 1937, the literary world faced the last stage of severe trials. Nationalist or anti-Japanese thought was not tolerated by the Japanese police, and the military encroached upon every literary activity. But writers did not succumb: instead they struggled to continue their art, and, most important, to preserve the Korean language. The best means at their disposal was the practice of pure poetry. Many of them retired to the country, following the example of the ancient hermits. Literary productions increased in the midst of spiritual and cultural crises. Between 1937 and 1941 more than fifty collections of verse adorned the literary world, a clear manifestation of the determined love of writers for the Korean language and a reaction against Japanese attempts to undermine what was truly Korean. The role played by the journals *Munjang* ("Literature," begun April, 1939) and *Inmun p'yŏngnon* ("Criticism of Culture," begun December, 1938) in the development of contemporary poetry should not be overlooked. Through these magazines poetry was furthered and new figures were brought to the attention of the public. The chief discovery of this period was of a cluster of nature and folk poets writing in the South with remarkable virtuosity.

In 1941 the Sino-Japanese war developed into the Pacific war, and the volunteer system (1938) of recruiting Koreans for the Japanese army was changed to a conscription system (1943). The Japanese, in order to suppress the identity of the Korean race, required Koreans to adopt Japanese names. Those who spoke the Korean language in public were seized and imprisoned.Two Korean newspapers were suspended on August 10, 1940, and the literary journals *Munjang* and *Inmun p'yŏngnon* were discontinued in April of the following year. Korean literature was driven underground. Writers in despair threw away their pens, and a dark period for literature ensued.

After the liberation in 1945 two movements came into being: one advocating the restoration of true Korean traditions and the other insisting on proletariat literature. Later these two groups were united; but because their activities tended to be more political than literary, an opposing group arose. Indeed, movements and countermovements appeared with bewildering rapidity in the brief span of three years (1945-1948), and amidst that confusion the "little magazines" were a formidable force where the conflicting beliefs and practices were explored and settled. Of a large number of verse collections published between 1945 and 1950, we must be content to pick out three representative titles to use as pegs on which to hang our discussion:[2] the *Ch'ŏngnok chip* ("Green Deer Anthology," 1946) by the "Southern Trio"; the *Saengmyŏng ŭi sŏ* ("The Book of Life," 1947) by Yu Ch'i-hwan; and the *Kwich'okto* ("The Cuckoo," 1947) by Sŏ Chŏng-ju.

Finding little nourishment in life under occupation and suppression, Pak Tu-jin and Pak Mogwŏl drew on their native South with its folklore and songs, and Cho Chi-hun on folk customs and Buddhist and court rituals. To them, however, the spiritual landscape symbolized by nature poetry was a veiled expression of nostalgia for the stolen country and of entreaty for its rapid return. Like pastoral poetry in the West, most of Pak Tu-jin's poems are allegorical pieces intended to cover his patriotic fervor or his vision of Prelapsarian life. In a chant to the sun as the source of life, Pak implores the sun to dispel the night of doubt and sorrow in order that he may enjoy once again the fellowship of man and nature. Pak Mogwŏl has not only the soul but also the art of a folk poet. His lines are bewitchingly subtle and simple, but it is the simplicity of a master craftsman who has hammered and chiseled every line into shining felicity. Cho Chi-hun is an equally, if not more, gifted technician. When he sent in a group of poems including the now famous *Sŭngmu* ("Monk Dance") to the magazine *Munjang,* its poetry editor, Chŏng Chi-yong, the best modern poet in Korea, is said to have marvelled at his mastery of language. Cho's, too, is a world of elegance and harmony where monks and court ladies dance a classic dance, vividly suggesting glimpses of past glory. The poetry of the "Southern Trio," though a poetry of withdrawal, possesses classical grace and elegance, precision and simplicity, reminiscent of the best *sijo* poems. Indeed, their lyrical gift, their lapidary style, and their haunting rhythm are seldom surpassed. Their achievement has remained influential in modern Korean poetry, for, like Chŏng Chi-yong, they have loved language for itself and taken poetry "further on its path."

Yu Ch'i-hwan's best poems are lucid yet symbolic, free from verbalism or condensation. He did not lead a poetic revolution but was content to find a style adequate to fit his vision. His images seldom shock or provoke, yet throughout his career he has shown a quiet control of his materials. Like the sunflower that defies the tyranny of the sun or the rock that ignores storm and wind, he sings fondly of a life of integrity and imperturbability, free from scepticism and sentimentality. As long as he has the sun and moon above him, he is content to die at any moment; yet for his enemy and those who flatter his

---

[2]Most of the poems in these collections were, however, written before 1945.

enemy he asks the sun and moon to avenge him. Indeed, he succeeds in giving a calm philosophic overtone to genuine feeling. This overtone is typically Confucian in its refusal to be fettered by the tribulations of mundane life or to be marred by the pursuit of name and fame.

Sŏ Chŏng-ju's verse is characterized by the freshness and simplicity of emotion. His earlier collection of verse depicts a decadent world full of lepers, snakes, musk incense, and country lasses. But in the *Kwich'okto,* he sought inspiration in such cultural remains as the Stone Cave Temple near the ancient Silla capital or in such Korean lore and myth as that of Ch'unhyang, that ravishing dancing girl whose feminine virtue gave rise to the best classical fiction in Korea. He is still attached to his own world, but a world this time of chrysanthemums and cranes, stone Buddhas and ruined monuments. There are seldom the agonies of self-consciousness or the torments of a divided man.

In sum, the post-liberation period belonged to the established poets, who drew upon the undying cyclical patterns of nature or the cultural heritage of the people. They fully recognized the events and temper of the time when doubt and frustration loomed dark and men despaired of imminent crises; but they left a new generation to wrestle with these problems.

The Korean War did not produce a Wilfred Owen or a Dylan Thomas,[3] but it effected a split between conventional and experimental expression. It produced a new generation that rejected the ruling poetic fashions and endeavored to reshape the poetic medium. The call for sacrifice was for them the opportunity of exorcism. The war probably helped to make the traditional poets, especially the poets in the *Green Deer* tradition, look out of date; for the war of 1950-1953 was the first modern war fought in Korea; it was a war for everyone, soldiers and schoolboys alike. The dilemma of the young writers in the early fifties is best reflected in the poets of the *Huban'gi* group.[4] This group vigorously repudiated the matter and manner of prewar verse, which no longer reflected the contemporary state of society or the disintegration of former values. Some began with a dire criticism of life in postwar Korea, scathingly analyzing the emptiness of modern man and illuminating their poems with bitter irony. Some intended to shock or provoke the reader into awareness of contemporary idiocies and abuses. Some fondly flirted with the unconscious or sought that "twilit realm of inmost being" in order to find metaphors and symbols for their work. In quiet succession, writer followed writer, with new themes, new accents, and new cadences.

Their works reflect a number of contemporary Western influences con-

---

[3]I have in mind Thomas' *A Refusal to Mourn the Death, by Fire, of a Child in London,* one of his "most touching lyrics."

[4]An avant-garde circle organized by a group of young poets in Pusan in September, 1952.

flicting with each other.[5] Their foremost concern, as far as I can judge, is that of style; the experimental and modernist movement they launched was a stylistic revolt that relentlessly pursued variety and individuality. But poverty of thought or shallowness of vision cannot be cloaked by a mere manipulation of texture. An introduction of a few Americanisms, some Existentialist vocabulary, or certain swear-words does not in itself constitute modernity. A comparison of an International Express with an IBM machine is nothing but a pastiche. Often experiments in form and language resulted only in flat and crude prose, the writing of which has been likened by Frost to playing tennis without a net. Although means alone cannot and should not become the sole preoccupation of poetry, some postwar poets are effecting a contribution to the modernization and revitalization of the Korean language. They are still grappling with time, and occasionally we glimpse their struggle to transcend the plight of the day. But it is too early to predict whether they are participating in the historical development of Korean poetry.

---

[5]For a convenient survey of contemporary verse in Korea see *Hanguk munhak chŏnjip*, XXXV (1959) and *Hanguk chŏnhu munje sijip* (1961).

XII. Twentieth-Century Literature: Prose

We have mentioned that the first "new" novel is the *Hyŏl ŭi nu,* published serially in 1906.[1] Strictly speaking, Yi In-jik's works[2] occupy the transitional period between the traditional historical romances or fantastic tales and the modern novel in the truest sense. Yet, in his conception of plot and characterization, in the good use of realistic prose and dialogue, Yi In-jik is a pioneer. He is the author of other major works: The *Kwi ŭi sŏng* ("The Voice of a Devil," 1906-1907),[3] *Ch'iaksan* ("Pheasant Hill," 1908),[4] and *Ŭnsegye* ("The Silver World," 1908). Another writer of importance is Yi Hae-jo (1869-1927), who is noted for his prolificacy. He is inferior to Yi In-jik in plot and description; most important, he lacked feeling for the new age. His works include the *Chayujong* ("The Liberty Bell," 1910), *Moranbyŏng* ("The Peony Screen," 1911), *Pip'asŏng* ("Sound of the Lute," 1913), and *Hwa ŭi hyŏl* ("The Blood of the Flowers," 1912).

Characteristically, the new novels were a literature of enlightenment which dealt with such themes as the political sovereignty of the people, promotion of education, criticism of early marriage by alliance, or the evils of superstition. Nevertheless, the new novels embraced several significant elements of the modern novel. They adopted a prose style which used the everyday language of the common people. Their subjects were chosen from contemporary life, and their scenes were set in the contemporary world. Their style became more descriptive than narrative, more analytical than chronological. Yet there were several contradictions in the new novels in the 1910's. They still followed the conventional theme of "the reproval of vice and promotion of virtue." In the *Kwi ui sŏng,* for instance, the villains who murder the heroine, Kilsun, and her child are punished at the end of the book. Also, the new novels still presented types rather than individuals. A stepmother, for example, was still represented as an evil person, and the *Ch'iaksan* suffers from such character-

---

[1]Published in book form in 1907. Its sequel, *Moran pong* ("Peony Peak"), was serialized in the *Maeil sinbo* in 1923.

[2]See Chŏn Kwang-yong, "Yi In-jik yŏn'gu," *STN,* VI (1957), 157-254 and Song Min-ho, "Kukch'o Yi In-jik ŭi sinsosŏl yŏn'gu" ("A Study of Yi In-jik's News Novels"), *Mulli nonjip,* V (1962), 1-47.

[3]Published in book form in 1908.

[4]According to the 1918 edition, this work consists of two parts, the second part appearing under the name of Kim Kyo-je.

ization. As a corollary of these shortcomings, the new novels were concerned chiefly with outcome, how they "came out." They were concluded with artificial and often melodramatic "happy endings" which would certainly have delighted those who read only the concluding chapter of a nineteenth-century novel. In short, the new novels contained defects in both form and content.

Yi Kwang-su[5] is truly the first writer of the modern novel in Korea. In 1915 Yi published the *Ŏrin pŏt ege* ("To Our Young Friends"). This story deplored the conventional marriage, declared that the Koreans had hitherto not loved, and preached love as the first step to marriage and enlightenment. Yi's other major works are the *Kaech'ŏkcha* ("The Pioneer"), *Mujŏng* ("The Heartless," 1917), and *Hŭlk* ("The Soil"). The motive of the first two works was, as the author later stated, to inspire national consciousness and to point the direction Korean youth should follow. In his later works he continuously preached love, the importance of education and enlightenment, racial consciousness, and patriotism. The influence of Buddhism and Tolstoyan humanism is apparent in his mature works. He also wrote historical novels. As a stylist Yi ranks among the greatest of Korean writers; the reader of his works is most impressed by their grand scale of conception and view of the world and life. His novels are rich in ideas and ideals. He conceived of literature as a political and social means of persuasion and enlightenment rather than a pure art. What writers of the next generation attacked was precisely this didactic function of literature that Yi upheld.

The young writers of the *Ch'angjo* circle advocated pure art in literature in defiance of Yi's "impure" motives in his works. The group preached that literature should present life as it is. They contributed a great deal to the establishment of colloquial prose style as a literary medium by differentiating the tenses and even by incorporating dialects. The most notable among them was Kim Tong-in (1900-1951), who wrote nearly a hundred short stories. Two characteristics mark his writings. They are inclined towards naturalism, and they strive for aestheticism, art for art's sake. The *Kwangyŏm sonat'a* ("Lunatic Flame Sonata") and *Kwanghwasa* ("The Mad Painter") remind the reader of Oscar Wilde; the *Kim Yŏnsil chŏn* ("Life of Kim Yŏnsil") resembles Maupassant's *Une Vie*. His preoccupation with psychological description led him to unjustified sensationalism or to emphasis on the sordid, gloomy, and sick.

The golden age of naturalism in Korea produced Yŏm sang-sŏp (1897-1963) and Hyŏng Chin-gŏn (1900-1943). Their activities centered around two journals, *Kaebyŏk* ("Creation") and *Chosŏn mundan* ("Korean Literary Circles").

Yŏm arrived on the scene in 1921 with the *P'yobonsil ŭi ch'ŏnggaeguri* ("The Green Frog in the Specimen Gallery"), which is often considered the first work of naturalism in Korea. His productive period was, however, between

[5]Cf. Kwak Hak-song and Pak Kye-ju, *Ch'unwŏn Yi Kwang-su* (1962).

1925 and 1933, when he published the *Chogŭman il* ("A Small Incident," 1926) and other longer novels. In these works he diagnosed his time and society by analysis, exact psychological investigation, and "scientific" documentation. The *Samdae* ("Three Generations") is one of his better novels.

Hyŏn is an uncontested master of the short story. His stories are noted for their mastery of technique, scenic description, use of the language of the lower class, and frank and vivid evocation of sexual desire. Despite his indebtedness to Maupassant and Zola, his characters are basically Korean, and his aim was, as he stated, "to grasp the soul of the Korean people." His stories include the *Halmŏni ŭi chugŏm* ("Death of the Grandmother," 1923), *Unsu chohŭn nal* ("A Lucky Day," 1924), *Pul* ("Fire," 1924), and *Sinmunji wa ch'ŏlch'ang* ("Newspapers and Iron Bars," 1929).

From a literary viewpoint, the "new trend" movement which began between 1923 and 1924 was a reaction against the romanticism which dominated the *Paekcho* group. It criticized these writers for their disregard of the masses and took as its theme the life of the lower classes, the miseries of the suffering mass. The works of this group often concluded with tragic and terrifying endings, usually with murder or arson. The best example of this type of writing is the *Kia wa sallyuk* ("Starvation and Murder," 1925), by Ch'oe Sŏhae (1901-1933). Working as a servant in a noodle shop, a porter, or as a revolutionary anti-Japanese fighter in Manchuria, Ch'oe was familiar with the life of the lower classes. His work is simple and concise as well as dynamic, as for example, in the description of the flood in the *K'ŭnmuljin twi* ("After the Flood," 1925). Pak Yŏng-hŭi (b. 1901) in the *Sanyangkkae* ("The Hunting Dog," 1925) and Chu Yo-sŏp (b. 1902) in the *Illyŏkkŏkkun* ("Ricksha Man," 1925) and *Sarin* ("Murder," 1925) show their sympathy toward this movement.

With the organization of the Korean Artist Proletariat Federation, the literature of the new trend school was developed into proletarian literature. Where it had dealt with poverty and resistance, it became strongly class-conscious. Advocates of proletarian literature therefore organized activities under a unified command and regarded literature as a means for the political ends of socialism. As writers became class-conscious and purpose-conscious, they emphasized content more than form. The *Naktong kang* ("The Naktong River," 1927), by Cho Myŏng-hŭi, is the first story dealing with the class struggle. Other writers known as sympathizers in this movement were Yu Chin-o (b. 1906), Yi Hyo-sŏk (1907-1942), Ch'ae Man-sik (1904-1950), and Han In-t'aek. Yu's *Yŏjikkong* ("Factory Women," 1931) and Yi's *Noryŏng kŭnhae* ("The Coast of the Russian Territory," 1931) are directly inspired by this movement. Yu's later novels, however, show his preoccupation with the sorrow and ennui of the intelligentsia in the thirties and forties. Later Yi Hyo-sŏk, too, changed his style, and in the *Ton* ("The Hog," 1933) and later works he dealt in lyrical prose with man's profound appreciation of, and often unity with, nature.

In fiction the thirties were perhaps the most productive decade, characterized by different schools and various trends. The spokesman for the disillusioned intellectual was Ch'ae Man-sik, who in the *Redimeidŭ insaeng* ("Ready-Made Life," 1934) outlined the history of the Korean intellectuals and the cause of their despair. Yi Hyo-sŏk and Yi T'ae-jun (b. 1904) proved themselves to be superlative craftsmen and masters of short stories. Kye Yong-muk (b. 1904), who began his career with realistic stories, changed his style after the *Paekch'i Adada* ("The Idiot Adada," 1935) and wrote chiefly in the tradition of art for art's sake. Kim Yu-jŏng (1908-1937) had a unique style and precise diction and demonstrated his talent in the *Sonakpi* ("The Shower," 1935), *Sankkol* ("Deep Mountain," 1935), and other stories. His works are rich in local color and satire. The characters of his stories are ignorant and simple peasants whose naïve joys and sorrows found wrily humorous expression through his pen.

While "naturalistic" realism stressed the objectivity and the ordinary aspects of experience, psychological realism portrayed the contents of the mind, the inner world. In the *Nalgae* ("The Wings," 1936), the representative work of psychological realism, Yi Sang (1912-1939) portrays the plight of a helpless intellectual tormented by pitiless self-analysis. The hero of the story is supported by his prostitute-wife and does nothing but play with his wife's toilet articles. In one of his idle speculations on life the hero exclaims that the sooner he gets off the fast revolving earth, the better he will be. In this and a later story, the *Chongsaeng ki* ("The End of Life," 1937), Yi's interest is in revealing character by closely tracing the hero's "unending and uneven flow of the mind."

Contrarily, another group of writers indulged in photographic reproduction of contemporary customs and events with understanding irony. In the *Ch'ŏnbyŏn p'unggyŏng* ("Scenes on the Riverside," 1936), Pak T'ae-wŏn (b. 1909) depicted contemporary scenes with the camera's eye, agreeable or disagreeable, but without any comment. The dialogues of women washing their clothes by the river, scenes of barber shops, and small incidents taking place on a corner street—Pak was indeed true to reality when he recorded all these in sober language.

A cluster of young writers who won recognition in the later thirties and early forties wrote their works during the last stage of Japanese domination. The best means at their disposal was the practice of pure literature. Whereas the established writers brooded over the present and dwelt on the memory of a freer past, young writers accepted reality as it was and tried to build up their literary careers without much ado. Kim Tong-ni (b. 1911) has his own theories to support his works. In the *Hwarang ŭi huye* ("The Posterity of the *Hwarang*," 1935), *Munyŏ to* ("Portrait of a Shaman," 1936), and *Pawi* ("The Rock," 1936), he depicted traditional Korean characters, realities, and emotions with a refined style. He drew his materials from the myths and legends of the South and handled them skillfully to give unity and coherence to his works. "However fantastic, unscientific, or supernatural a phenomenon may be," he declared, "it can be 'real' in a work of art if transformed and lived into an organic whole." Mysticism and the Taoist idea of nothingness permeate his early works. In the *Sŏnangdang* ("The Sŏnang Hall," 1937) Chŏng pi-sŏk (b. 1911) delved deeply into nature and re-created a primitive and vigorous world rich in local color. His pantheistic fervor and nature worship put him in the line of Kim Tong-ni. When, however, he turned from nature to the urban middle class, he became interested in the description of sex and nudity. In the *Soŭi* ("The White Dress," 1939) Kim Yŏng-su also demonstrated his skill in the description of sexual desires and nudity. Other writers of importance before the outbreak of the Pacific war were An Su-gil (b. 1911), Hwang Sun-wŏn (b. 1915), Ch'oe In-uk (b. 1920), Kwak Ha-sin (b. 1920), Ch'oe T'ae-ŭng (b. 1917), and Im Og-in (b. 1913).

The 1940's were a dark period in all branches of literature, owing to the Japanese suppression of all writings in the Korean language. The political confusion after 1945 and the subsequent outbreak of the Korean war also disrupted creative activities. Although some works of artistic merit were produced, most efforts during the conflict were accounts of the horror and devastation of war. Meanwhile a series of significant events took place in the literary world. In 1954 the Korean Academy of Arts was established, and the Korean Chapter of the P.E.N. was organized to promote cultural exchanges with the West. Several literary awards were instituted, and increasing opportunities were offered to writers by new literary journals, such as the *Munye* ("Literature," 1949), *Sasanggye* ("The Thinking World," 1953), *Munhak yesul* ("Literary Arts," 1954), *Hyŏndae munhak* ("Contemporary Literature", 1955), and *Chayu munhak* ("Free Literature," 1956).

Perhaps the most important change that took place in the postwar Korean literary world was the emergence of a new generation in the late fifties. Most of them, born between the twenties and thirties, experienced the horror of war as students and later as soldiers. The freedom and peace which returned to Korea in 1945 proved not to have returned at all. Far from being able to enjoy the fruits of the liberation, Korea faced a more formidable and insoluble problem than ever before in her history: division of the country. Less than two years after the birth of the First Republic, the war erupted. The Armistice, however, in failing to bring about unification, only added a new set of problems. Conscious of the political, social, and moral chaos caused by the war and its aftermath, a cluster of young writers rose to repudiate this chaotic world and to challenge the ruling literary fashions and conventions.

Literary moods, modes, and themes popular in Korean fiction till the early fifties were merely the fag-ends of earlier literary movements in Europe. Untroubled by current anxieties that faced the new generation and uninformed of modern innovations in fiction—such as in form, sequence, and point of view—

established writers still wrote in the realistic and naturalistic tradition. To them the novel was still a mere fictional narrative of characters, following closely the rules of plot, character, and setting. This was, however, not entirely their fault. The wholesale assault of Japanese colonialism, whose ultimate goal was the obliteration of the Korean language, not only bred conservatism but prevented the modernization of the language. Shut off from the outside world and being under the vigilant surveillance of the military police, the realistic and naturalistic technique, with an emphasis on moods and anecdotes, was then perhaps best suited to their works. Their chief concern was story, conceived in chronological terms. What the new generation discovered was the inner world of the protagonist, his psychological and philosophical dimension, in fine, his stream of consciousness.[6] Sceptical of inherited techniques and established reputations, the new writers subjected the leading names and achievements in modern Korean fiction to a fresh valuation. They freed Korean fiction from its well-knit formalism and made it a medium adequate to contain the quality of complex, contemporary experiences. Indeed, they have driven the last nail into the coffins of Balzac and Zola and enthroned Camus, Hemingway, and Sartre as their new gods.

The publication of the *Hanguk chŏnhu munje chakp'um chip,* the first anthology of postwar Korean fiction, heralded a new epoch. The twenty-one stories that make up the book were written between 1955 and 1960.[7] The editors have separated the wheat from the chaff in this bountiful harvest of new fiction; hence the selections evidence vigor, variety, and creativity. What the young writers have in common is a fierce concern with the exploration of the new condition of man. Their material may be the untidy, shabby, and incoherent pattern of everyday life; but they are not afraid to delve into the most secret chamber of the unconscious and to communicate their findings. One work depicts the isolation of the individual amidst a mechanical, dehumanized civilization and his futile quest for freedom; a second, which recounts the career of a family, tries to discover archetypal patterns in the Collective Unconscious of the Korean people; a third reveals the perplexity and doubt of modern man incapable of personal salvation; a fourth describes the history of a club, an asylum of the Beat Generation in Korea, where "new barbarians" escape from the banality and horror of city life; a fifth recounts in short sentences, reminiscent of Hemingway and Camus, the morning's doings and thoughts of two persons, a man who has received a draft notice and his wife; a sixth probes the individual's pathological situations such as sexual and inferiority complexes.

What is new here is that they have grasped Time in the Bergsonian sense

[6]For a discussion of the stream of consciousness in Western literature see Robert Humphrey, *Stream of Consciousness in the Modern Novel* (Berkeley and Los Angeles, 1954).

[7]For a study of three new writers see Kim Sang-sŏn, "Sinsedae non" ("A Study of the New Generation"), *KK*, 23 (1961), 21-79.

and have discovered new techniques and new forms adequate to express their new vision. To this end they have resorted to the symbolist technique, where meaning emerges not from discourse alone (which only gives a hint) but rather from a weaving of such devices as image, symbol, and pattern. In the *Yohan sijip* (1955), for example, a prison camp is a symbol of the modern world where a quest for freedom and dignity costs man his life. Within the confines of barbed wires, as Garcian declares in *Huis Clos,* "L'Enfer c'est les Autres." Just as the central image in *A Passage to India* is the Marabar caves, so that in the *Pulkkot* (1957)[8] is a cave, a symbol for the dark night of society. In this cave, Ko Hyŏn, the protagonist, lies wounded by a bullet from a fellow villager, now a turncoat communist. The villager had also shot and killed Hyŏn's grandfather when he refused to entice his grandson to come out of the cave. It was in the same cave that Hyŏn's father, a leader of the Independence Movement (1919), spent his last night before he died of bullet wounds received from the Japanese police. Amidst the pang of wound and anguish of solitude, his interior monologue reveals his many-leveled flow of experience, a life of escape, indecision, and vacillation. He is tormented by the thought of his father's cruel death, of the unhappy life of his mother—especially the pain in her thigh and knee resulting from torture at the hands of the Japanese, of his escape from the Japanese army in North China, of his wanderings in South Manchuria, of his frustrating career as a teacher at a girl's school upon his return to Korea after the liberation, and of his inability to love Miss Cho, a fellow school teacher. Surrounded by a chain of mountains and valleys, a symbol of flux, Hyŏn is a wave tossed up and down as his stream of consciousness carries him back to the past. In the end, Hyŏn wins against the void and abyss in himself. Dawn assails the cave, scattering his despair and humiliation and crowning society's endless struggles for freedom and integrity with hope and determination. *Le Temps perdu* of his thirty years of life finally becomes *le Temps retrouvé.* Here the author has arranged his material in such a way that the career of three generations in Hyŏn's family becomes a symbolic picture of the life of the Korean people during the past fifty years.

This is only one of the advances made by the new writers in an attempt to renew both the form and substance of Korean fiction. The communication of stream of consciousness requires a subtler technique, for the underlying realities of an individual's consciousness can be revealed only by new techniques in expression. All of the new writers are trying in their various ways to discover new styles and techniques and to give a renewed vision of reality. They may vary in point of view or approach, but they affirm their function as writers in a contemporary society to make us a little more aware of the world we live in

[8]Cf. Frederick H. Dustin, "An Aspect of Korean Contemporary Literature with Special Reference to *Bulggot,"* unpublished M. A. thesis, University of Washington, 1958. For the translation of the story see pp. 23-102.

and to convey to us new reality and new vision. Modern Korean fiction, at its beginning, was at least one hundred years behind its Western counterpart. It is now abreast of all developments in fiction and the arts abroad; it should not be too long until Korean literature, both verse and prose, becomes a part of world literature.

Bibliography: *Twentieth-Century Literature*

Cho Yun-je, *Hanguk munhak sa* (1963), pp. 393-599.
Paek Ch'ŏl, *Sinmunhak sajo sa* ("Trends in the New Literature") (1953).
Yi Pyŏng-gi and Paek Ch'ŏl, *Kungmunhak chŏnsa* ("Complete History of Korean Literature") (1958), pp. 211-450.

Collections

Hanguk munhaksang susang chakp'um chŏnjip ("A Collection of Award-Winning Verse and Prose") (5 vols.; 1961-1963).
Hanguk siin chŏnjip ("A Collection of Modern Korean Verse") (10 vols.; 1959-).
Hanguk sinjak munhak chŏnjip ("A Collection of Current Korean Literature") (10 vols.; 1963).
Hanguk tanp'yŏn sosŏl chŏnjip ("A Collection of Modern Korean Short Stories") (3 vols.; 1958).
Hanguk yŏksa sosŏl chŏnjip ("A Collection of Modern Korean Historical Novels") (12 vols.; 1960-1961).
  (1) Yi Kwang-su, (2) Kim Tong-in, (3) Hyŏn Chin-gŏn, (4) Yun Paeng-nam, (5) Pak Chong-hwa, (6) Kim P'albong, (7) Hong Hyomin, (8) Kim Tong-ni, (9) Chang Tŏk-sang, (10) Ch'oe In-uk, (11) Pak Yong-gu, (12) Chŏng Han-suk.
Hyŏndae Chosŏn munhak chŏnjip ("A Collection of Contemporary Korean Verse and Prose") (7 vols.; 1938).
  (1) verse, (2-4) short stories, (5) essays, (6) drama, (7) criticism.
Hyŏndae Chosŏn changp'yŏn sosŏl chŏnjip ("A Collection of Contemporary Korean Novels") (10 vols.; 1936-1937).
  (1-2) Yi Ki-yŏng, (3) Yi Kwang-su, (4) Yi T'ae-jun, (5) Yŏm Sang-sŏp, (6) Kim Ki-jin, (7) Ham Tae-hun, (8) Chang Hyŏk-chu, (9-10) Sim Hun.
Paek Ch'ŏl *et al.*, eds., *Hanguk chŏnhu munje chakp'um chip* ("A Collection of Postwar Korean Prose") (1960).
Paek Ch'ŏl *et al.*, eds., *Hanguk chŏnhu munje sijip* ("A Collection of Postwar Korean Verse") (1961).
Pak Chong-hwa *et al.*, eds., *Hanguk munhak chŏnjip* ("A Collection of Modern Korean Literature") (36 vols.; 1958-1960).
Yi Hyo-sŏk, *Hyosŏk chŏnjip* ("Collected Works of Yi Hyo-sŏk") (5 vols.; 1959-1960).
Yi Kwang-su, *Ch'unwŏn mun'go* ("Collected Works of Yi Kwang-su") (24 vols.; 1959-).
Yi Sang, *Yi Sang chŏnjip* ("Collected Works of Yi Sang") (3 vols.; 1958-1959).

Translations

Cho Byung Hwa, *Before Love Fades Away,* tr. Kimg Dong Sung (1957).
Korean P.E.N. Club, ed., *Collected Short Stories from Korea,* I (1961).
Korean Poets Association, ed., *Korean Verses* (1961).
Lee, Peter H., *Anthology of Korean Poetry,* pp. 161-179.

Zŏng In-sŏb, tr., *A Pageant of Korean Poetry* (1963), pp. 61-248.
_____, tr., *Modern Short Stories from Korea* (1958).
A Chapbook of Contemporary Asian Poetry of *The Beloit Poetry Journal,* XIII, No. 2 (Winter 1962-1963), contains translations from modern Korean poems on pp. 29-34.
A group of modern Korean poems also appeared in *Die Stimme des Menschen: Briefe und Aufzeichnungen aus der ganzen Welt 1939-1945* (Munich, 1961), pp. 79, 356-357, 368-369, 506-507.

Works Written in Western Languages

Kang Younghill, *The Grass Roof* (New York, 1931).
Kim, Richard E., *The Martyred* (New York, 1964).
Kim Yong Ik, *The Diving Gourd* (New York, 1962).
_____, *Love in Winter* (1963).
Li Mirok, *Der Yalu Fliesst* (Munich, 1946), *The Yalu Flows: A Korean Childhood,* tr. H. A. Hammelmann (East Lansing, 1956).

Comparative Chronology

Korea		The West

B.C.

2333	Tangun myth		
	Majigut (Puyŏ)	c.800	Homer
	Saebŭlk (Koguryŏ)	c.700	Early Greek cyclic poets
	Hanbŭkch'um (Ye)	fl. c.600	Sappho
		c.518-443	Pindar
	Festivals in the 5th and 10th	c.500	Heraclitus
	months (southern tribes)	469-395	Socrates
		427-348	Plato
108	Yŏok: *Konghuin*	384-322	Aristotle
		70-19	Virgil
17	King Nuri: *Hwangjo ka*	65-8	Horace

A.D.

28	Anon.: *Tonnorae*		
32	Anon.: *Aso kok*		
42	Anon.: *Kujibong yŏngsin ka*		
c.24-57	Anon.: *Saenae ak*	c.40-104	Martial
c.57-80	Anon.: *Tara ak*		
c.80-112	Anon.: *Chia ak*		
c.196-230	Anon.: *Samae ak*		
	Anon.: *Mulgyeja ka*		
c.356-402	Anon.: *Kamu*		
c.417-458	King Nulchi: *Uso ak*		
	Anon.: *Ch'isullyŏng kok*		
c.458-479	Paekkyŏl: *Tae ak*		
c.479-500	Anon.: *Taldo ka*		
c.500-514	Anon.: *Kanin*		
c.514-540	Anon.: *Miji ak*		
c.540-576	Anon.: *Toryŏng ka*		
c.579-632	Master Yungch'ŏn: *Hyesŏng ka*		
	Anon.: *Narhyŏnin*		
	Sirhye: *Sirhye ka*		
c.600	King Mu: *Mattung yo*		
c.635	Anon.: *P'ungyo*		
c.654-661	Anon.: *Yangsan ka*		
	Wŏnhyo: *Muae ka*	fl.670	Caedmon

Korea		The West
c.661-681	Kwangdŏk: *Wŏnwangsaeng ka*	
692	Sŏl Ch'ong systematized the *idu*	
c.699-702	Siro: *Mo Taemara ka*	
c.702-737	An Old Man: *Hŏnhwa ka*	c.700 *Hildebrandslied* 709 Aldhelm d.
737	Sinch'ung: *Wŏn'ga*	c.730 *Beowulf*
c.742-765	Anon.: *Sanhwa ka* Master Wŏlmyŏng: *Che mangmae ka* Master Ch'ungdam: *Ch'an Kilborang ka* Hŭimyŏng: *To Ch'ŏnsugwanŭm ka*	
760	Master Wŏlmyŏng: *Tonnorae*	
765	Master Ch'ungdam: *Anmin ka*	
c.785-798	King Wŏnsŏng: *Sin'gong sanoe ka* Yŏngjae: *Ujŏk ka*	
c.826-836	King Hŭngdŏk: *Aengmu ka*	804 Alcuin d.
c.861-875	Anon.: *Hyŏn'gŭmp'o kok* Anon.: *Taedo kok* Anon.: *Mun'gun kok*	
879	Ch'ŏyong: *Ch'ŏyong ka*	
888	*Samdaemok* compiled	891 *The Anglo-Saxon Chronicle*
915	Ch'oe Ch'i-wŏn d.: *Kyewŏn p'ilgyŏng (chip); Fa-tsang ho-shang chuan*	
c.924-927	Anon.: *Pŏnhwa kok*	
c.927-935	Sinhoe: *Mangguk aega*	
c.965-967	Great Master Kyunyŏ: Eleven devotional poems	c.975 *The Exeter Book* c.955-1020 Aelfric 991 *Battle of Maldon*
1021	King Hyŏnjong: *Hyŏnhwasa piŭmgi*	
1068	Ch'oe Ch'ung d.	1079 Abélard b.
1096	Pak Il-lyang d.	
		1100 *Chanson de Roland*
1120	King Yejong: *To ijang ka*	1126 Guilhelm IX d.: the earliest known Provençal trouba-
1146	Kim Pu-sik: *Samguk sagi*	dour
c.1151-1170	Chŏng Sŏ: *Chŏng Kwajŏng*	
1170	Im Ch'un d.: *Kuksun chŏn*	

Korea		The West	
1214	Yi In-no: *P'ahan chip*	c.1200-1205	*Niebelungenlied*
1215	Kakhun: *Haedong kosŭng chŏn*	c.1200-1225	Walter von der Vogelweide
1241	Yi Kyu-bo d.: *Paegun sosŏl; Tongguk Yisangguk chip* (2nd ed.: 1251)	c.1250	*Owl and the Nightingale Sumer ist icumen in*
1254	Ch'oe Cha: *Pohan chip*		
c.1214-1259	*Hallim pyŏlgok* composed		
		c.1230-1280	Guillaume de Lorris & Jean de Meung: *Roman de la Rose*
c.1285	Iryŏn: *Samguk yusa*		
	Anonymous Koryŏ songs composed in the 13th and 14th centuries	1265	Dante b.
		c.1291	Dante: *Vita Nuova*
		c.1304-1307	Dante: *Convivio; De Vulgari Eloquentia*
1306	An Hyang d.	c.1300-1321	Dante: *Commedia*
		1304	Petrarch b.
c.1330	An Ch'uk: *Kwandong & Chukkye pyŏlgok*		
1340	Ch'ae Hong-ch'ŏl d.: *Chahadong*		
1342	U T'ak d. Yi Che-hyŏn: *Yŏgong p'aesŏl*	c.1348-1358	Boccaccio: *Decameron*
1351	Yi Kok d.: *Chukpuin chon; Kajŏng chip*		
1363	Yi Che-hyŏn: *Ikchae chip*	c.1360-1399	Langland: *The Vision concerning Piers the Plowman*
1367	Yi Che-hyŏn d.		
1392	Chŏng Mong-ju d.: *Tansim ka*	c.1387-1400	Chaucer: *The Canterbury Tales*
1393	Chŏng To-jŏn: *Monggŭmch'ŏk; Suborok; Napssi ka; Chŏng tongbang kok*		
1394	Chŏng To-jŏn: *Sindo ka*		
1395	Chŏng To-jŏn: *Mundŏk ka* Kwŏn Kŭn: eulogies		
1398	Chŏng To-jŏn: *Sindo p'algyŏng si*		
1402	Ha Yun: eulogies		
1405	Yi Ch'ŏm d.: *Chŏng Sija chŏn*		
1414	Ha Yun: eulogies		
1419	Pyŏn Kye-ryang: eulogy		
1420	Pyŏn Kye-ryang: *Ch'uksŏngsu; Sŏngdŏk ka*		
1425	Pyŏn Kye-ryang: *Hwasan pyŏlgok*		

Korea		The West	
1431	Maeng Sa-sŏng d.: *Kangho sasi ka*	1431	Villon b.
1433	Collec. of folk songs begun		
1436	Yun Hoe d.: *Ponghwangŭm*		
1443	King Sejong invents the *han'gŭl*		
1444	Chŏngŭmch'ŏng tr. *Ku-chin yün-hui*		
1445	*Yongbi ŏch'ŏn ka* compiled		
1446	King Sejong promulgates the *han'gŭl*		
1447	Annotations on the *Yongi ŏch'ŏn ka* completed		
	Prince Suyang comp. *Sŏkpo sangjŏl*		
	King Sejong: *Wŏrin ch'ŏn'-gang chigok* (-1448)		
	Sin Suk-chu ed. *Tongguk chŏngun*		
1449	*Sŏkpo sangjŏl* and *Wŏrin ch'ŏn'gang chigok* printed		
1451	Kim Chong-sŏ *et al.*: *Koryŏ sa*		
1454	*Sejong Annals* completed		
1458	Pak Yŏn d.		
1459	*Wŏrin sŏkpo* published		
1462	Sejo tr. *Lankavatara sūtra*		
1464	Kim Su-on tr. *Diamond sūtra*		
		1469	Malory: *Le Morte d'Arthur*
1477	Sŏ Kŏ-jŏng: *T'aep'yŏng hanhwa kolgye chŏn*	1478	Sir Thomas More b.
	(pub. about 1482)	c.1478	First book printed at Oxford
1481	No Sa-sin: *Tongguk yŏji sŭngnam*		
	Chŏng Kŭg-in: *Sangch'un kok*		
1489	Sŏ Kŏ-jŏng d.: *Tongguk t'onggam; P'irwŏn*	1489	Villon: *Le Grand Testament; Le Petit Testament*
	chapki; Tongin sihwa	1492	Columbus discovers the West Indies
1493	Sŏng Hyŏn: *Akhak kwebŏm*		
	Kim Si-sŭp d.: *Kŭmo sinhwa*		
		1498	Vasco da Gama discovers sea-route to India
c.1504	Anon.: *Siyong hyangak po*		
		1516	More: *Utopia*
c.1506-1544	Hwang Chin-i		Ariosto: *Orlando Furioso*
		1519	Leonardo da Vinci d.
1527	Ch'oe Se-jin: *Hunmong chahoe*	1532	Rabelais: *Pantagruel*
1543	Chu Se-bung establishes the first private academy	1534	Rabelais: *Gargantua*

Korea		The West
1548 Yi Hyŏn-bo: *Ŏbu ka*		
	1549	Du Bellay: *La Défence et Illustration de la langue française*
1565 Yi Hwang: *Tosan sibi kok*	1564	Shakespeare b.
		Marlowe b.
		Michaelangelo d.
c.1510-1569 Pak Chun ed. *Akchang kasa*		
	1572	Camoëns: *Os Lusiados*
1577 Yi I: *Kosan kugok ka*		
1580 Chŏng Ch'ŏl: *Kwandong*	1580	Montaigne: *Essais*
pyŏlgok	1581	Tasso: *Gerusalemme Liberata*
1585-1587 Chŏng Ch'ŏl: *Sa miin kok; Sok miin kok; Sŏngsan pyŏlgok*		
1587 Kwŏn Ho-mun d.: *Tongnak p'algok*		
Im Che d.: *Hwasa*		
1589 Hŏ Nansŏrhŏn d.: *Pong-sŏnhwa; Kyuwŏn ka*	1590	Spenser: *Faerie Queene*, i-iii
	1595	Sidney: *Defence of Poesy*
1598 Pak In-no: *T'aep'yŏng sa*		
	1600	Caldéron de Barca b.
1605 Pak In-no: *Sŏnsangt'an*	1605	Cervantes: *Don Quixote*, I
1611 Pak In-no: *Saje kok; Nuhang sa*	1611	Authorized Version of the Bible
1612 Kwŏn P'il d.		
1614 Yi Su-gwang: *Chibong yusŏl*		
1615 Ch'a Ch'ŏn-no d.	1615	Cervantes: *Don Quixote* II
	1616	Shakespeare d.
		Cervantes d.
1618 Hŏ Kyun d.: *Hong Kiltong chŏn*		
Yi Hang-bok d.		
1628 Sin Hŭm d.: *Sangch'on chip*		
1629 Cho Chon-sŏng d.: *Hoa kok*		
c.1630 Anon.: *Kyech'uk ilgi*	1631	Donne d.
	1633	Herbert d.
1635 Pak In-no: *Yŏngnam ka*		
Yi Chŏng-gu d.: *Wŏlsa chip*		
1637 Yi An-nul d.	1637	Corneille: *Le Cid*
Kim Sang-yong d.		Descartes: *Discours de la Méthode*
1638 Chang Yu d.	1638	Milton: *Lycidas*
c.1642-1645 Yun Sŏn-do: *Sanjung sin'gok*		

	Korea		The West
1645	Yi Myŏng-han: d.		
	Yun Sŏn-do: *At the Begin-*		
	ning of the Feast; At the		
	End of the Feast		
1647	Yi Sik d.	1649	Crashaw d.
1651	Yun Sŏn-do: *Ŏbu sasi sa*		
1652	Kim Sang-hŏn d.		
1656	Kim Kwang-uk d.		
1658	Kim Yuk d.		
1659	Prince Pongnim (King	1666	Molière: *Le Misanthrope*
	Hyojong) d.	1667	Milton: *Paradise Lost*
		1668	Dryden: *Essay of*
			Dramatick Poesie
		1670	Pascal: *Pensées*
1673	Yu Hyŏng-wŏn d.:		
	Pan'gye surok	1674	Boileau: *L'Art Poétique*
		1677	Racine: *Phèdre*
		1678	Bunyan: *Pilgrim's Progress*
c.1687-1688	Kim Man-jung: *Kuun mong*		
c.1689-1692	Kim Man-jung: *Sassi*		
	namjŏng ki	1690	Locke: *Essay concerning*
			Human Understanding
c.1700	Anon.: *Inhyŏn wanghu chŏn*	1700	Dryden d.
1711	Nam Ku-man d.	1711	Pope: *Essay on Criticism*
		1719	Defoe: *Robinson Crusoe*
1720	Chu Ŭi-sik d.		
c.1725	Anon.: *Kwandŭng ka*		
		1726	Swift: *Gulliver's Travels*
			Thomson: *The Seasons*
			(-1730)
1728	Kim Ch'ŏn-t'aek ed.	1728	Pope: *Dunciad*
	Ch'ŏnggu yŏngŏn	1755	Johnson: *English*
			Dictionary
		1759	Voltaire: *Candide*
		1751-1776	*L'Encyclopédie*
1763	Kim Su-jang ed. *Haedong*		
	kayo		
1764	Yi Ik d.	1764-1770	Rousseau: *Les Confessions*
	Kim In-gyŏm: *Iltong*		
	changyu ka		
	Anon.: *Kogŭm kagok*		
1766	Yi Chŏng-bo d.	1766	Lessing: *Laokoon*
		1767	Herder: *Fragmente*
		1774	Goethe: *Werther*
c.1777-1800	Anon.: *Ch'unhyang chŏn*	1778	Herder: *Volkslieder*
		1781	Kant: *Kritik der Reinen*
			Vernunft
		1788	Kant: *Kritik der Praktis-*
			chen Vernunft

Korea		The West
	1789	Blake: *Songs of Innocence*
	1795	Goethe: *Wilhelm Meisters Lehrjahre*
	1797	Hölderlin: *Hyperion*
	1798	Wordsworth and Coleridge: *Lyrical Ballads*
	1800	2d ed. of *Lyrical Ballads* with Preface
	1803	Alfieri d.
1805 Princess Hyegyŏng: *Hanjung nok*	1805	Schiller d.
Pak Chi-wŏn d.: short stories	1808	Goethe: *Faust*, I
	1810	Madame de Staël: *De L'Allemagne*
1817 Chŏng Yag-yong: *Kyŏngse yup'yo*	1817	Coleridge: *Biographia Literaria*
		Keats: *Poems*
1818 Chŏng Yag-yong: *Mongmin simsŏ*	1819	Schopenhauer: *Die Welt als Wille und Vorstellung*
	1820	Lamartine: *Méditations*
	1821	Keats d.
	1822	Shelley d.
1824 Yu Hŭi: *Ŏnmun chi*	1824	Byron d.
	1832	Goethe: *Faust*, II
	1835	Carducci b.
	1837	Leopardi d.
1844 Anon.: *Hanyang ka*	1844	Dumas: *Les Trois Mousquetaires*
1845 Sin Wi d.: *Chaha chip*		
1846 *Namhun t'aep'yŏng ka*		
	1850	Hawthorne: *The Scarlet Letter*
		Wordsworth d.
	1851	Melville: *Moby Dick*
1853 Kim Chin-hyŏng: *Pukch'ŏn ka*	1854	Thoreau: *Walden*
	1855	Whitman: *Leaves of Grass*
	1856	Flaubert: *Madame Bovary*
	1857	Baudelaire: *Fleurs du Mal*
	1859	Darwin: *Origin of Species*
	1865-1872	Tolstoy: *War and Peace*
1866 Hong Sun-hak: *Yŏnhaeng ka*	1866	Dostoevsky: *Crime and Punishment*
	1867	Marx: *Das Kapital*
	1875-1876	Tolstoy: *Anna Karenina*
1876 Pak Hyo-gwan and An Min-yŏng eds. *Kagok wŏllyu*	1876	Mallarmé: *L'Après-midi d'un Faune*
	1880	Dostoevsky: *The Brothers Karamazov*

Korea		The West
1883 Chŏng Yag-yong's *Yŏyu-dang chŏnso* published	1883	Nietzsche: *Also Sprach Zarathustra*
1884 Sin Chae-hyo d.: *p'ansori* texts	1884	Mark Twain: *Huckleberry Finn*
	1885	Hugo d.
1906 Yi In-jik: *Hyŏl ŭi nu*		
1908 Ch'oe Nam-sŏn edits *Sonyŏn* Pak Yong-dae, *et al.*: *Chŭngbo munhŏn pigo*	1908	Yeats: *Collected Works*, I, II
	1909	Gide: *La Porte étroite*
1910 Chu Si-gyŏng: *Kugŏ munpŏp*	1910	Gide: *La Symphonie pastorale*
	1913	Proust: *A la Recherche du Temps perdu* (-1928)
1915 Yi Kwang-su: *Ŏrin pŏt ege*	1917	Valéry: *La Jeune Parque*
1918 *Ch'angjo*		
1922 *Tonga Daily*		
1920 *P'yehŏ; Kaebyŏk*		
1921 Han'gŭl hakhoe organized		
1922 *Paekcho*	1922	Joyce: *Ulysses*
Kim Sowŏl: *Chindallaekkot*		Yeats: *Later Poems*
		Valéry: *Charmes*
		Eliot: *The Waste Land*
1923 *Kŭmsŏng*	1923	Rilke: *Duineser Elegien; Sonette an Orpheus*
	1924	Breton: *Manifeste du Surréalisme*
1925 K.A.P.F. (-1935)	1925	Kafka: *Der Prozess*
	1926	Kafka: *Das Schloss* Rilke d.
1933 Ch'oe Sŏhae d.	1933	Malraux: *La Condition Humaine*
1934 Chindan Society organized		
1934 Kim Sowŏl d.		
	1935	Eliot: *Murder in the Cathedral*
1936 Yi Sang: *Nalgae*		
1937 Sim Hun d.		
1938 *Inmun p'yŏngnon*	1938	Sartre: *La Nausée*
1939 *Munjang*	1939	Yeats d.
		Joyce: *Finnegans Wake*
		Frost: *Collected Poems*
1941 Chŏng Chi-yong: *Paengnoktam*		
1942 Yi Hyo-sŏk d.	1942	Camus: *L'Etranger*
1943 Yi Yun-jae d. in Hamhŭng prison	1943	Hesse: *Das Glasperlenspiel* Eliot: *Four Quartets*
1944 Yi Yuksa d.	1944	Sartre: *Huis-Clos*
Han Yong-un d.		
1945 Yun Tong-ju d. in Fukuoka prison	1946	Camus: *La Peste*
	1949	Faulkner receives the Nobel prize
1951 Kim Tong-in d.		
	1950	Eliot: *The Cocktail Party*

	Korea		The West
1952	Pang Chong-hyŏn d.	1952	Proust's *Jean Santeuil* pub.
	Huban'gi group organized		
1953	*Sasanggye*		
1954	Korean Academy of	1954	Hemingway receives the
	Arts organized		Nobel prize
	Korean Chapter of the		
	P.E.N. organized		
1955	*Hyŏndae munhak*		
1956	*Chayu munhak*		
1957	Ch'oe Nam-sŏn d.	1957	Faulkner: *The Town*
1960	*Hanguk chŏnhu munje*	1958	Eng. tr. of *Dr. Zhivago*
	chakp'um chip	1960	Camus d.
1961	*Hanguk chŏnhu munje sijip*	1961	Hemingway d.
		1962	Ponge: *Le Grand Recueil*
			Char: *La Parole en Archipel*
			Faulkner d.
		1963	Frost d.

GLOSSARY & INDEX

I. Personal Names

II. Other Proper Names & Titles

ABOUT THE AUTHOR

PETER H[acksoo] LEE is widely regarded as the foremost modern interpreter of Korean culture and literature to the West. He was educated at Seoul, Yale, Fribourg, Florence, Oxford, and Munich, where he received his Ph.D. in 1958. Dr. Lee has been a Fellow of the American Council of Learned Societies and the Bollingen Foundation. His publications include *Studies in the Saenaennorae* (Rome, 1959), *Kranich am Meer: Koreanische Gedichte* (Munich, 1959), and *Anthology of Korean Poetry* (New York, 1964). Currently he is preparing the first complete translation of the *Haedong kosŭng chŏn* ("Lives of Eminent Korean Monks," 1215) and *Yongbi ŏch'ŏn ka* ("Hymns to Flying Dragons in Heaven," 1445). He has taught at Yale, Columbia, and the University of Hawaii, where he is Associate Professor of Korean Language & Literature.